HINDSIGHT

HINDSIGHT

IN SEARCH OF
LOST WILDERNESS

JENNA WATT

First published in 2022 by
Birlinn Limited
West Newington House
10 Newington Road
Edinburgh
EH9 1QS

www.birlinn.co.uk

ISBN 978 1 78027 745 5

British Library Cataloguing-in-Publication Data
A catalogue record of this book is available on request from the
British Library.

Typeset by Initial Typesetting Services, Edinburgh

Papers used by Birlinn are from well-managed forests
and other responsible sources.

Printed and bound by Clays Ltd, Elcograf S.p.A.

To my family,
past and present.

Contents

To aim for the highest point is not the only way to climb a mountain.

– Nan Shepherd

1

The Stalk, Part One

I won't shoot her.

It's my first thought as I wake up.

Reluctantly, I push back the warm duvet. I turn on the side light, lie back on the bed and stare at the ceiling. Take a moment to remember where I am – in a canal cottage holiday rental in Banavie, near Fort William. It's early on a Friday morning in November 2019. I didn't get much sleep – worst-case scenarios continually played out in my dreams, and I woke up every hour thinking I'd slept in. My stomach is tight with the knowledge of what the day holds. Today I'll be participating, for the first time, in Scotland's deer cull.

I take a deep breath, slowly exhale and push the heel of my hand into my diaphragm to bring some relief. I get up and dress in the layers of clothes I laid out last night. I gently open the bedroom door and tiptoe quietly down the old stairs. Siouxsie, my eighteen-month-old rescue dog, follows me into the kitchen, hoping for some semblance of her normal routine in this strange new place. The linoleum floor is freezing cold. I quietly potter about in my socks, making our breakfasts. Upstairs, in the other room, my friend sleeps. She agreed to come along and look after Siouxsie while I do the stalk. I imagine their day: pleasant walks along Neptune's Staircase in the crisp winter air and cuddles by the wood fire. I consider cancelling

1

and staying with them instead, but it's too short notice, I'm here now. While the kettle boils, I take Siouxsie out into the garden. It's silent except for the gentle burble of water coming from the locks. I round the corner of the building and watch Siouxsie pad across the frost, leaving a trail of little paw prints as she does a slow patrol of the boundary fence. Everything is still. I take her for a quick walk along part of the canal, more for my benefit than hers. We pass through the back gate and onto the towpath, which sparkles with ice crystals. I can see my own breath in the cold air. The sky is a beautiful clear dark blue and still dotted with stars. Partially silhouetted against the sky, I can see the outline of Ben Nevis's northwestern face. At 1,345 metres, it is Scotland's highest mountain. Against the dark blue, the first snow is visible on its rounded peaks, giving the impression of a thin place.

Ben Wyvis, another mountain, was visible from my family home, a constant on the horizon. For as long as I can remember, I appreciated the first snow on the ben, its reassuring appearance marking the onset of winter. Over the following weeks the snow line would gradually travel down its south face and spread across the Black Isle towards Inverness. On this November morning, it doesn't occur to me yet how the first snow will impact the day ahead.

Siouxsie and I return to the house and have our respective breakfasts. I sit at the table and consider how other people must behave on the morning of a stalk. I can't help but imagine middle-aged white men in Barbours, eating their cooked breakfasts, smiling and rubbing their hands together, looking forward to an invigorating day of sport on the hill; meanwhile, I sit alone, in a strange place, wondering why I thought this would be a good idea. I collect my lunch and thermos off the table and head out to defrost the car and load my gear. Sitting on the passenger seat in my tightly packed waterproof bag are my snacks, gaiters, a change of clothes, my digital recorder and my blue inhaler. Waiting for me at the estate is a hired rifle with ammo.

Dawn breaks, and I need to get on the road. My friend comes downstairs to say goodbye, scoops up Siouxsie and waves at me from the door. I wish I wasn't going alone, but the cost was too prohibitive to take someone with me. I wonder what state I'll be in when I return, whether it will have changed me in some way or whether I'll have gone through with it at all. I don't want to leave, but I'm ready.

'It's an adventure!' I tell myself, but it does little to loosen the knot in my stomach.

In the months and weeks leading up to the stalk, I've been growing more and more anxious. Some of this anxiety stems from the concern that the stalk might be too physically challenging, but it's mainly about feeling pressured into taking the shot. I emailed a few gamekeepers when planning this trip to ask what would happen if I didn't go through with it. This was mostly met with dismissive assurances that they could set me up in a suitable shooting position. But the opportunity to shoot was never a concern – it was my own resolve that I was worried about.

I've been reading journal articles, books, government guidelines and reports on the subject of the deer cull. I've even attended events where heated discussions around deer-management practices have arisen, usually amongst those same middle-aged white men. But I wondered whether the people writing these articles or those with strong opinions on cull numbers had ever necessarily participated in the deer cull themselves. I wanted to know what it was like to be on the hill, what it meant to undertake the cull. I'd heard that the estate I was heading to was committed to meeting culling targets.

The deer cull in Scotland is administered by around 44 voluntary deer-management groups, normally made up of land managers, landowners and/or gamekeepers from estates or land holdings within a specific geographical area. Each DGM carries out an annual count of deer numbers across their location and agrees a cull target that takes into consideration the carrying capacity of the environment, compatibility with other land uses and the needs of the local economy. Some estates commit to keeping their deer numbers even lower per square kilometre if they have urgent objectives, such as tree regeneration. Nature Scot, previously Scottish Natural Heritage, is the public body that provides advice to the DGMs; it also conducts its own deer counts, targets, research and sometimes interventions. The cull itself is not a public activity – the majority of culling is conducted by professional stalkers and, of course, by landowners and their guests on sporting estates.

Hind stalking is not something that is normally accessible to the likes of me. It requires significant disposable income, means of accessing sometimes remote estates, some level of stamina and physical ability as well as an acceptance of the desired outcome. I'm a self-employed woman with a chronic illness, and I've never had a desire to hunt. I accepted stalking as the preserve of wealthy landowners and tourists wishing to experience a quintessential Highland pursuit. Until recently, I never seriously considered my identity as a Highlander in relation to the cultural significance of deer, despite the stag being Scotland's emblematic species for centuries.

I was intimidated by the fact that deer stalking was male-dominated, but I decided to confront that anxiety head-on. I wanted to understand the role of women in deer stalking and land management by experiencing the environments they work in for myself, though my stalk would be a one-off, and I would be a client. I made a conscious choice to go hind stalking rather than stag stalking for a number of reasons: hind stalking is more effective for conservation purposes, I didn't want there to be a trophy aspect to the stalk, and it was more affordable at half the price.

It's essential for me as an artist to viscerally experience the themes of my work. I'm drawn to places of ideological conflict, to putting myself in situations where I can experience physical adversity and engage with the different tensions and polarised views within any debate. In these places I often find we can gain a deeper understanding of our own humanity. I sometimes see my role as an impartial observer, creating and designing spaces and narratives as a kind of middle ground that can host the complexity of these tensions. I knew I could experience ideological conflict in those few seconds before choosing whether or not to pull the trigger. As the stalk approached, I didn't know for certain what I would decide, but I made a promise to myself that, should I find a hind in my sights, even with expectation heavy around me, I had permission not to take the shot.

*

As I drive further away from Fort William towards Spean Bridge, I eventually lose the signal on my phone. The little blue dot on the satnav follows me optimistically but not with total certainty. Maybe I'll get lost and miss the stalk? But I know I'll never let that happen, not after the effort that's gone into planning this trip. I'd rather turn up late than not at all.

I don't know this area of Scotland particularly well. I'm usually rushing through Fort William to catch a ferry to the Hebrides, but I now find myself on the northeastern side of Ben Nevis, though it's no longer in view. I pass through an array of land uses and habitats – uplands, peatland, rough grazing, grassland, forest plantations, ancient woodland, native woodland, freshwater lochs and hydroelectric schemes. I continue to drive through the mosaic of landscapes, and, as I do, I think about the other estates that I'd considered stalking with. Occasionally I only got as far as the homepage on their website before ruling them out. From the beginning, I was determined to stalk at an estate that held the same environmental principles as me. I wanted to ensure the cost of the stalk was going to support an estate with what I deemed at the time to be 'good' land practices such as habitat restoration and/or species reintroduction. I was particularly determined to avoid anywhere that practised driven grouse shooting, mainly because this can sometimes include illegal raptor persecution, mountain-hare trapping and muirburn, when old growth is burnt off on a moor. These management practices are commonly used to ensure a high grouse population, which ensures a large number of birds to flush for driven shooting. This form of grouse shooting requires more intense land management compared to walk-up grouse shooting, in which dogs flush the birds and there are fewer guns – and therefore fewer birds shot. Driven grouse shooting is fast becoming unpopular with the public and environmentalists. In 2020, the Scottish Government announced a move to ban grouse shooting on estates where there were known illegal killings of birds of prey and other wildlife crimes. Instead, a licensing scheme for grouse shooting would be introduced. Despite this seemingly positive news, the debate continues to rage between gaming estates and environmental groups, with one prioritising fragile rural economies and the other the fragile biodiversity of our uplands.

Quite apart from the ethical issues at stake, I experience acute feelings of ecological and climate grief, so stalking in a landscape that was suffering from poor biodiversity as a result of land management practices could have an impact on my mental wellbeing. I wanted nothing to do with it.

Not long into my search, I found somewhere that appeared to meet my criteria: Corrour Estate, 23,000 hectares on the edge of Rannoch Moor with 'an abundance of wildlife' and its own environmental fact sheet. Encouraged that this might be the one, I continued researching. The landowner, Dr Lisbet Rausing, had previously received some criticism from the Scottish gaming community for publicly deriding the practice of grouse shooting. She was also criticised for being Swedish, rich and a woman. I warmed to her immediately. Dr Rausing's sister Sigrid Rausing at Coignafearn Estate had also voiced her concerns regarding the management of sporting estates. The sisters had taken on the endeavour to prove that land could be managed for both game and conservation on their respective estates.

*

The little blue dot follows me as I finally turn off before Loch Laggan onto the B-road that leads onto the Corrour estate. The satnav says I still have another 30 minutes until I reach my destination. That's a long driveway. The sun has risen, but much of the hillsides are still in shadow. Frost glimmers on the moor grasses. As I head further into the estate I see signs warning me of logging activity in the area, and I feel a little disappointed. I'd hoped to pass through broadleaf woodland, not commercial conifers and cleared plantations. According to the Corrour environmental report, much of this logging work is being undertaken to undo some of the damage caused by the forestry policy that existed up until 1984 and saw native and ancient woodland replaced by conifers. Now these forests are being managed to make way for native trees and to create a new woodland with a mix of species, densities and ages of trees. This supports ecological niches within appropriate environments. As well as intentional reforestation and planting, natural regeneration is also occurring, meaning native woodland on the estate has increased since 1995 from 39 hectares to 259 hectares.

As I continue to drive, I reach an area of cleared plantation, a bare square surrounded on three sides by conifers, and in the middle of the clearing I spot a wooden high-seat blind for shooting deer. The sight of the blind immediately piques my already heightened level of anxiety. I haven't been told what kind of terrain we will be stalking on, or for how long. I assumed I'd be walking on a hillside, maybe with a small troop of men. I have certainly not imagined sitting crammed in a hide with rifles positioned as if defending an outpost. I'm also not certain of how many people typically go on a deer stalk; surely enough to make it financially viable for the estate – maybe three? Though the more people on the hill, surely the harder the stalk. I keep reminding myself this isn't driven grouse shooting. There will be no beaters, no line of guns waiting. As for how long it will take, we'll surely have to stop at sunset, which gives us at least six or seven stalking hours. The Corrour website states that we'll be stalking 'truly wild deer, the old-fashioned way'. I'm not sure what they mean by 'truly wild' or exactly how 'old-fashioned' the stalk will be. Maybe it means going out with ponies.

Much of the Corrour Estate is part of Nature Scot's Wild Land Areas. Though not a statutory designation, Scotland's 42 Wild Land Areas (WLAs) are deemed to be national assets because they reflect our contemporary perception of semi-natural landscapes. The WLAs encompass some of Scotland's most popular tourism sites, including the Cuillin on Skye, the Three Sisters of Glencoe, the Cairngorms and Ben Nevis. Nature Scot's methodology for mapping these WLAs provides an interesting insight into how we perceive wildness or naturalness. Bodies of water, whether salt, fresh, loch or sea, rate very highly, along with bog and mountain environments. Even different species of tree can impact our perception of wildness, with broadleaf species outclassing conifers, and felled woodland having a low rating. Ultimately though, the WLAs have four main attributes: they are perceived by us as being natural, the landscape is rugged, they are at a distance from public roads, and there are no pylons or modern buildings. A WLA designation is not solely based on remoteness or visible infrastructure, though. It also reflects an area's capacity for wildlife, its effects on human wellbeing and its economic impact. The concept of wildness or wilderness is understandably another contentious subject, especially in Scotland's rural communities, many of which continue to struggle with contemporary drivers of depopulation. Some might look at these 'remote' areas and think they're empty, untouched, wild, or even describe them as being in 'the middle of nowhere', but the land is or has been managed by people in some way. I personally don't consider any parts of Scotland to be wild, and I see every place as being in the middle of somewhere. To describe them as 'untouched', for example, erases the history of generations of people who lived and worked on the land at one time.

*

I expected a little more detail to be sent through once the stalk had been arranged, but nothing ever came. I had previously been ghosted by a few estates after telling them who I was and what I was doing, so I was just happy to have received confirmation. In an effort to feel prepared, I reached out to a young woman I follow on Instagram. She worked at the time as a ghillie on an estate adjacent to Corrour. I asked her what to expect and what to wear. She recommended everything that's sitting in my kit bag now, but also, if I wanted, my own knife, for the gralloch. Once I'd looked up what the gralloch was, I quickly determined that I would not be bringing my own knife. The gralloch is the act of disembowelling the deer after it's been shot, leaving the less valuable organs for other species to consume and making the carcass lighter for carrying off the hill. If I'm not committing to pulling the trigger, I certainly won't be gralloching the quarry.

I'm forced to stop as I meet a tall metal gate with an electronic keypad. There's no camera or assistance button. Well, this is it, I think. I don't remember being told about a gate, and I don't have the code.

Before giving up and turning back, I check my emails. Still no signal. Fortunately I have taken a picture of my correspondence with the estate. There *is* a code after all. I tap it into the keypad; after a moment there's a buzzing sound and the gate opens. No turning back now. The conifer plantation abruptly ends, giving way to an unexpectedly epic and mostly treeless landscape. I cautiously follow the single-track road as Loch Ghuilbinn comes into view, and I'm at once overshadowed by the Grahams, Corbetts and Munros that rise up around me[*]: Meall nan Caorach, Chno Dearg, Aonach Beag and Beinn Eibhinn, which, using my very limited Gaelic, appears to mean

---

[*] In Scotland, a Graham is a mountain with a height of between 2,000 to 2,500 feet (609 to 762 metres), a Corbett is over 2,500 feet (763 metres), and a Munro is a mountain with a height of more than 3,000 feet (914.4 metres).

'funny' or 'happy mountain'. I hadn't accounted for Corrour Estate having its own Munros, which in hindsight was a glaring omission in my research. If I had realised, I might have been a little more persistent in understanding the details of the stalk in fear of having to summit one. I'm aware that the prospect of being able to access 20 Munros from Courror would be thrilling to your avid hill walker. However, a Munro-bagger I am not.

Above one of the Grahams, I spot a bird of prey. I slow right down and watch it as it catches a thermal pocket and soars around the hill. I look for defining features – widely splayed wing tips, long broad wings, brown underside: it could be an eagle. I like to assume everything's an eagle. Although I'm fairly good at spotting birds of prey, I'm terrible at identifying them. I make a mental note to find an RSPB identifier chart for the glove compartment. As I follow the raptor around the hill, I can see it's flown straight into an unkindness of ravens. Four or five of them swoop and dart at the bird, relentlessly pestering it. There must be a food source nearby.

I pass them and unconsciously begin to quote one of Lady Macbeth's well-known monologues:

> The raven himself is hoarse
> That croaks the fatal entrance of Duncan
> Under my battlements. Come, you spirits
> That tend on mortal thoughts, unsex me here,
> And fill me from the crown to the toe top-full
> Of direst cruelty!

The buildings that make up Corrour Estate come into view, and at this moment, much like King Duncan, I have little idea what's about to unfold.

I slowly approach some beautiful Victorian stone buildings surrounded by broadleaf trees. Nobody's around, so I pull up outside what could be a steading. I can see there's a lane that leads to a cobblestone courtyard, and I spot a Land Rover with an all-terrain vehicle loaded in a trailer. This must be the place. I've been instructed to meet the head stalker, Allan, at the larder, but I have no idea which of these buildings that would be. All of them look like they could be guest accommodation. I get out of the car with my kit and put on my walking boots. This is it, I think to myself, as I slip the gaiters up my calves and attach them to my boots. I consciously surrender to whatever the rest of the day might bring, sling my backpack on and wander up the lane to the courtyard. I notice a faintly familiar odour: it's musky, maybe earthy, strong and distinct. In an almost Proustian way, it evokes something, but I put that thought aside as a man, whom I assume is Allan, strides across the courtyard to greet me.

He's tall and friendly with a reassuringly local accent and is wearing a fairly traditional stalking outfit – wool plus-fours, gaiters and a deerstalker hat. His attire is definitely in keeping with what you would expect from a deer stalker, but it does make me reflect on what the difference is between a costume and a uniform. Regardless, it makes the stalk feel very formal and serious, which is as it should be, given what's involved.

'How was the drive over?' Allan asks.

'Beautiful. I think I saw an eagle.'

Allan, interested in the sighting but sceptical, says, 'Could have been, but we have buzzards too.'

Unable to dispute this, I have to accept that it probably was a buzzard. I take a quick look around the courtyard. It's quiet, empty, except for a dog kennel. There's no troop of enthusiastic stalkers standing around with rifles – maybe they've not arrived yet or are in another building finishing their cooked breakfast.

'Is anyone else coming?' I ask with some trepidation.

'It's just us and Ethan,' says Allan. Ethan's our ghillie.

I wonder if this scenario, which I find out later is quite typical, is better or worse than what I was imagining. At least in a group I could blend into the background or chat to people about why they were on the stalk. On my own, I'll feel much more exposed and quite shy. And I'll definitely be confronted with pulling the trigger.

Ethan stealthily appears in the courtyard, seemingly from nowhere. He's a young, friendly guy, dressed in more contemporary stalking gear.

A ghillie is a person who acts as an attendant during the stalk. It's usually a seasonal role carried out by a younger person who might be learning the practice of stalking. Ethan doesn't speak much, but I don't think ghillies are supposed to talk to clients unless spoken to first. I'm a client now. This dynamic always makes me feel deeply uncomfortable, firstly because I'm very rarely a client of anyone, and secondly because I find this sort of deference inherently classist. It feels a little like I'm being asked to play a role today, one where I'm from a different social background, and I'd rather we just didn't. This dynamic only exacerbates my concern at there being just three of us. In fact, I start to feel a kind of pressure, the pressure of expectation.

'Have you stalked before?' asks Allan.

'No, first time,' I reply.

'Let me show you.' He signals for me to follow him into one of the buildings.

We enter a very small, slightly chaotic office space, the only source of natural light being the entranceway. The smell from earlier is even stronger here.

'This is where you want to aim.' Allan points to an illustrated poster stuck to the wall. It has pictures of deer from all angles with heart-shaped blobs marked on the translucent bodies. These show the optimum bullet placement for a clean kill. We're straight into business, I realise, and I study the illustrations.

'We'll try to get one in this position, with its right flank exposed.' Allan points to one of the deer.

'Best to split this section from knee to shoulder into thirds, and aim for the top of the middle third here.' I nod confidently. That seems clear enough, but I steal a moment to take in as much detail as possible. If I go through with it, it has to be a clean kill. I couldn't live with myself if it wasn't.

We head back out to the courtyard, and Allan tells me to jump in the Land Rover. I automatically go to open a back door, but I'm redirected to the front seat. Clients go in the front, ghillies in the back, naturally. I hop in and look back at Ethan and smile. I notice the rifle's sitting in its own soft case across his lap. This is the first time I see the rifle. I'm surprised Allan doesn't have one too, but I say nothing. Ethan politely smiles back at me. It sinks in then, the situation that I've just put myself in; I'm being taken somewhere – I don't know where exactly, or for how long – with two men I don't know, and a rifle. I've been conditioned to fear and avoid this kind of situation in every other context, but I'm just supposed to be okay with it now. I repress every instinct I have to run away, telling myself that it's all fine, because it is, it really is. I seriously regret not bringing my friend with me. Not because I feel in danger, but because they could cover the awkward silence as all the colour drains from my face. Allan puts the Land Rover into gear and says, 'Right, time for target practice.'

2

Discovering

Feral

One afternoon in 2017, while working a freelance job at the Macrobert Arts Centre just outside Stirling, I found myself with some time to kill. My interest in the environment and deer management had been growing, so I went to the university bookshop to peruse the shelves of the environmental studies section. Among the tall spines of the academic texts nestled a much smaller book. I pulled it out and turned it over in my hands. The cover showed a curious photograph of a stag standing in a mundane concrete high-rise car park, gazing out of a mesh-covered window. *Feral*, by George Monbiot. Drawn to the image of the stag – yes, I did judge a book by its cover – I took it to the counter.

Over the next few weeks, *Feral* became my go-to read as I commuted between Scotland's cities. Speeding through the country's green belt, book in hand, taking in each page, I became more and more aware of the farms and livestock, the swathes of land reserved for the 'white plagues' of sheep, as Monbiot referred to them. Concepts such as 'trophic cascade' and 'rewilding' set my imagination ablaze. I read about the wolves of Yellowstone, the excavation of Trafalgar Square, the return of Caledonian pinewoods to Scotland by Trees for Life, the Knapdale beavers and the potential for wolves at Alladale in the North Highlands. I couldn't believe the Highlands, my home, was at the forefront of such ambitious ecological restoration and species reintroduction. Page after page challenged my understanding of the landscape I grew up in. I learned more about Scotland's land use from Monbiot's book than I had during any of my own schooling.

Feral ignited a fire in me, an insatiable desire to understand the story of the land in my country: not just rewilding, but also gamekeeping, farming and tourism. I devoured nature books and articles, particularly ones about Scotland. So hungry was I to understand the dynamics and interrelationships of land management, conservation and economics, that I returned to university as a mature student to study Sustainable Rural Development. I became a member of the John Muir Trust and used my time off to visit various sites around Scotland that I'd either read about during my studies or in nature books – places designated as Sites of Special Scientific Interest, Special Areas of Conservation or Special Protection Areas. For fun, I'd meet High Life Highland rangers and asked them about the habitats they managed. I'd pour over Scotland's online Environment Map, picking locations I might visit, exploring the different map layers, discovering more designations, peat depths and potential wildcat reintroduction sites. I even engaged in a bit of citizen science, logging any red or grey squirrel sightings online. My fascination with sustainability and its interplay with land and conservation led to me writing my research dissertation on the environmental impact of the North Coast 500 or NC500, a 500-mile-ish route around the North Highlands, through some of Scotland's most beautiful and fragile environments and communities. I soon graduated, and I continued to feed my obsession, but academic texts, conferences and site visits were no longer enough. Unfortunately, I couldn't afford to participate in the working holidays run by organisations like Trees for Life or do volunteer path restoration work with the John Muir Trust or Nature Scot. I had to find other ways to satisfy the restlessness within me. Eventually I acknowledged a gentle pull I'd felt towards something that you can't volunteer for, something that much of Scotland's ecological restoration depends on. For years I'd rationalised that the feeling was a response to my recent studies. But the gentle pull became taut as I realised I was being drawn towards a particular species, a species that had been vilified, a species that was central to conservation work in Scotland. Deer.

My mind was made up: I needed to participate in the deer cull.

The Conference

It was September 2019, and I was back at Stirling University for the inaugural Scotland: The Big Picture conference. The event brought together speakers and organisations at the forefront of ecological restoration and rewilding so they could share their varying approaches to habitat restoration and species reintroduction.

As I arrived at the Macrobert Arts Centre, it was clear from the long queue to get into the conference just how popular the discussion around rewilding was. Eventually I reached the front of the queue and showed my tickets to the polite but clearly frazzled person crossing names off a list. The building was full of researchers, scientists, land managers, farmers, rewilding advocates and even landowners, and I spotted more than a few familiar faces both from the rewilding movement and academia. The conference was about to start, so I was directed straight to the auditorium. We were in the main house, and it was packed to the back wall. I knew from my work in theatre that it could hold around 480 people. Impressive. I found a seat high up in the auditorium and took a look around the audience. The room was filled with white, able-bodied people. I turned to the person next to me, whom I happened to recognise from another conference, and shared my observation about the lack of diversity in the room.

'Oh yes,' they replied. 'It's very difficult to get landowners in the room.'

I paused as I noted our differing interpretations of diversity and considered their point. I wondered if this was always an issue in this context, the absentee landowner living up to the trope.

The person next to me scanned the room.

'It's good to see Anders here though,' they said.

'Anders . . . Povlsen?' I asked.

'Yes, he's sitting over there.'

To my total surprise, there he was. Anders Povlsen, one of the largest private landowners in Scotland, was sitting a couple of seats away on the other side of me, beside his director of conservation and forestry.

Povlsen, a Danish billionaire, is the UK's largest private landowner and owns multiple Scottish estates totalling over 90,000 hectares. These include Kinloch, Ben Loyal and Hope and Melness in Sutherland in the North Highlands; Braeroy and Tulloch, adjacent to Corrour on its northern boundary and separated by the River Spean; and Killiehuntly and Glenfeshie in the Cairngorms National Park. At around 17,000 hectares, Glenfeshie is one of Povlsen's larger estates. It is also part of Wildland, a project partner in the large-scale conservation project Cairngorms Connect. In 2021, Povlsen was ranked at number 161 on the Forbes 400 list. He owns retail chain

Bestseller, which has eleven fast-fashion brands under its name, including Vero Moda, Only and Jack & Jones, as well as significant stakes in Asos and Klarna.

I casually looked over at Povlsen. I never thought I'd be in a room with him. He was dressed in black from head to toe, in a shirt, trousers and black boots. I wondered if I should take this opportunity to introduce myself, maybe ask a question. I started to construct a question in my head, but before I had worked up the courage to go over, the lights went down in the auditorium and I was off the hook.

The conference began with an introduction from The Big Picture's director Peter Cairns. He welcomed everyone and gave a shout-out to some of the people in the room, including MSP Andy Wightman, who waved from much lower down in the auditorium. I couldn't help but wonder if Povlsen and Wightman had ever had a conversation. Cairns then went on to make a speech where he unashamedly reclaimed the term 'rewilding'. He made clear that rewilding was not about the reintroduction of wolves, as the media would have us believe. Rather, it was about restoring ecosystems and improving biodiversity with habitat corridors and species reintroduction. It was a strong message from Scotland's first charity dedicated to promoting, supporting and enabling rewilding.

Scotland: The Big Picture seeks to bring rewilding into mainstream conservation. It does this in a number of ways: creating campaigns and documentary films, supporting a network of smaller-scale rewilding projects, publishing books with essays about rewilding, undertaking feasibility studies for reintroduction of species such as lynx, hosting rewilding retreats, conferences and outreach and building networks of rewilding projects.

Despite Cairns's strong effort to break the association of

'rewilding' with the wolf, other terms such as ecological restoration and re-naturalisation remain widely used. For some, these terms are a better reflection of shared objectives and avoid the problematic use of 'wild' in 'rewilding'. Many object to the assumption that rewilding involves returning nature to a more 'wild' condition at all. I could appreciate these perspectives, but I wasn't ready to surrender the enthusiasm I had for such an ambitious term just yet.

The reason for this disassociation was not lost on anyone at the conference. All in the room were well aware of Alladale, and in particular Paul Lister, who purchased Alladale Estate, now Alladale Wilderness Reserve, in the north Highlands, 40 miles north of Inverness, in 2003. Soon after that he became known as the 'wolfman' of the Highlands for his controversial plan to reintroduce wolves to Alladale. When I talk about Alladale or Lister with friends, they won't usually know what or who I'm talking about until I use his moniker.

Although the media went wild for his bold statement of intent, neighbouring traditional sporting estates were perhaps concerned about the impact of wolves on deer numbers. The reserve experimented with introducing other species such as elk and wild boar, and it is home to a Scottish wildcat-breeding programme in partnership with the Royal Zoological Society of Scotland (RZSS). This is in addition to planting close to a million trees, restoring peatland, translocating red squirrels and building aquaponic gardens.

Alladale no longer offers commercial stalking as an activity, but instead encourages a luxury brand of ecotourism. The reintroduction of wolves isn't totally off the cards, but the project is now being put aside to prioritise other aspects of ecological restoration.

*

The morning presentations were well underway. Author David Hetherington provided some interesting insights into the lynx and the potential for Scotland as its home. Its one-time presence in Scotland was evidenced during the excavation of the Inchnadamph Bone Caves, along with the remains of a brown bear, wolf, arctic fox and polar bear. The intention behind rewilding lynx, as with most species reintroduction, is to restore an ecological process that's been identified as missing.

Hetherington talked eloquently about the challenges facing the lynx but also about their behaviour as a predatory species. Much like wolves, lynx prey on woodland species such as deer, meaning they could naturally reduce Scotland's deer numbers whilst assisting in the regeneration of native woodland.

During the morning break, I noticed Sophie and Louise Ramsay from Bamff in Perthshire, known for its private reintroduction of beavers. In early 2021, the estate launched its Bamff Wildland project, led by Sophie Ramsay. The intention of the project was to enable the land to regenerate itself, putting nature back in charge. This plan involved planting trees and wildflowers, creating more ponds, removing invasive non-native species and joining up habitats. As well as the Bamff Wildland project, the estate has an ecotourism business, with a mix of accommodation, one of which, the Hideaway, overlooks their active beaver pond.

After the break, Sir John Lister-Kaye from Aigas Field Centre took to the stage. I have very fond memories of visiting Aigas on a school trip, so I listened intently to what he had to say. He shared his belief, after working in conservation for over 50 years, that nature reserves were not the right approach. That creating detached, independent habitats didn't serve the wider ecology of our landscapes. To hear someone with his standing in conservation talk honestly about getting things wrong was hugely impactful. He was now advocating for landscape-scale restoration projects and wildlife corridors.

It was soon lunchtime. The audience seemed energised, and conversations spontaneously erupted all around me. I left the main auditorium, and I made a point of sitting outside after a morning in the dark theatre. It was a warm, sunny September day, and the campus always looked so good at this time of year. I found a grassy spot under an oak tree beside the loch to eat my packed lunch and watch the local waterfowl. It was really quiet, the sort of quiet you perhaps wouldn't associate with a university campus. Only a few people passed on the bridge above me as I sat and reflected on the morning's presentations. Speaker after speaker had come on stage and brilliantly advocated for their projects and habitats. All the presentations were inspiring in their own ways, but I was tired of listening to white men. Only four women appeared across the day, and, of them, only Lynn Cassells of Lynbreck Croft had been given a presentation slot. Two were confined to a panel, and the last was given the stage during the lunch break. Of course, that's not to say that more women weren't asked to present at the conference, but with only one woman out of eleven main speakers, the lack of gender parity was alarming.

I finished my lunch, and, as I gathered together my bits and pieces, I noticed an acorn on the grass. It was green, freshly dropped from its mother oak. I picked it up and noticed another beside it, then another. The ground was covered with them. I'd never tried to grow a tree before, but in the spirit of the day, I packed three acorns safely in my backpack.

I forfeited the afternoon's sunshine and headed into the dark theatre for the rest of the presentations. More inspiring talks were given, and Lynn Cassells was particularly engaging. She detailed how at Lynbreck they farm *with* nature on their

60 hectares. So alluring was their approach that I was tempted to do one of their courses.

Jeremy Roberts of the Cairngorms Connect partnership was also at the conference. I had seen his presentation before, but I never tired of it. Cairngorms Connect is a large-scale, 200-year conservation project situated within the Cairngorms National Park that focuses on delivering conservation objectives, including habitat restoration through native woodland regeneration, species control such as deer management and peatland restoration. While some of Cairngorms Connect's work aligns with the objectives of rewilding, it prefers the term ecological restoration. Interestingly, Cairngorms Connect is partially funded through the Endangered Landscapes Programme, which is supported by Arcadia, the charitable fund of Lisbet Rausing of Corrour.

The last presentation of the day was by Sean Gerrity from the American Prairie Reserve, a project based in Montana in the western United States that aims to protect the grasslands of the American prairies. In 2005 the reserve reintroduced a herd of bison to the grasslands, in part to protect the species, but also to reestablish their role in the grassland ecosystem. It was an impactful presentation, and Gerrity deftly illustrated how the project overcame opposition and eventually gained the support of neighbouring ranchers. What was most impressive was the scale of the restoration that was underway, but they had ambitions to make it even larger.

Gerrity's presentation concluded with a Q&A. Thoughtful questions were asked and good responses given, and then from down in the stalls, nearer the stage, a hand had shot up. A man stood up and, rather than wait for a mic, called out, 'What about the indigenous people?'

They were unable to hear him onstage, but I heard him at the back of the auditorium. A microphone was rushed to him.

'What about the indigenous people? Do they have a say in what you're doing?'

Gerrity looked a little taken aback. Maybe he hadn't expected a question like this outside of the US. He assured us that they had strong links with the local tribal communities and were in consultation. Though Gerrity's response was sufficient, it didn't adequately resolve the issues around what had been introduced into the room: the concept of neocolonialism.

Steve Micklewright, the CEO of Trees for Life, took to the lectern for the last item on the conference agenda, an introduction and invitation to join the Scottish Rewilding Alliance, a coalition of organisations, charities, businesses and groups with a focus on rewilding. Micklewright described the aims of the Alliance and listed those who were already signed up. They varied from big-name conservation charities, high-profile rewilding estates and family-based farms with a focus on conservation to rescue and walking groups. Although it sounded useful, I struggled to understand its role, other than as a network of projects and organisations. This became clearer in 2020, when the Alliance commissioned market research into public attitudes towards rewilding. It found that 76 per cent of the 1,000 people surveyed were in favour of rewilding in Scotland. The Alliance also petitioned the Scottish Government in 2019 for an amendment to a bill which would safeguard the future of wild beavers in Scotland, which was sadly unsuccessful at the time. However, under the same Animal and Wildlife Act, mountain hares were given more protection. Eighteen months later, in February 2021, the Rewilding Alliance launched a new campaign calling on the Scottish Government to declare Scotland as the world's first Rewilding Nation. They asked that 30 per cent of Scotland's land and sea be rewilded by 2030. The campaign launch was watched live online by over

2,500 people, with many attending from across the world. This was testament to the growing popularity of rewilding – or at least to the accessibility of the online launch event.

Steve Micklewright took over as CEO of Trees for Life after its founder Alan Watson Featherstone stepped down in 2017. Founded as an independent charity in 1993, Trees for Life might be one of the oldest rewilding or ecological restoration organisations in Scotland. Its focus is reforestation, in particular the restoration of Scots pine. In 2008, the charity bought Dundreggan Estate, which held some of the most important remaining fragments of Scotland's ancient Caledonian forest. Dundreggan is now home to a tree nursery of Scots pine, aspen, willow and birch. The charity has reintroduced red squirrels to the estate, reforested parts of Glen Affric, successfully introduced trees species at a higher altitude than thought possible in Scotland, advocated for the protection of beavers, hosted popular tree-planting working holidays and hopes to be the site of the world's first rewilding centre by 2022. In 2021, it launched Affric Highlands, which joined Rewilding Europe's network with an ambitious 30-year project to rewild over 200,000 hectares of the Scottish Highlands in partnership with local landowners.

The conference closed on what felt like a wave of optimism and chatter. People flooded out of the auditorium, and as I moved through the building, I saw roll-up banners being taken down, books packed away and people gathered in small groups to have their own debriefs. I left feeling tired and satiated. But as I headed back to Glasgow, a question from earlier in the day echoed in my thoughts. *What about the indigenous people?*

Women Stalkers

Leading up to my stalk, I had started following a handful

of Scotland's stalkers and ghillies on social media, mainly Instagram. My timeline gradually filled with images of landscapes from less accessible areas of Scotland and the more macabre aspects of stalking. The posts varied in tone; some documented the field signs of a particular species, celebrated an encounter or showed their quarry – quarry being a term for a hunted animal. But occasionally, they would share images of other species that they were required to hunt too, such as the fox. I found these images harder to look at. Sometimes deeply respectful, sometimes gory, and sometimes just shy of a 'grab and grin' image, these posts were confronting. I would console myself by remembering that these hunts were not akin to a traditional fox hunt with its brutality and pomp.

Following both men and women stalkers and ghillies, I observed what appeared to be a gender-based etiquette around the presentation of any quarry. Women stalkers and ghillies rarely posted pictures of themselves with their quarry. They mostly documented live animals, landscapes, their kit, or occasionally quarry with unusual or interesting features. Their captions were respectful, informative and supportive of this way of life and gave an insight into the practice of stalking and deer management. The grids of male stalkers, however, had a slightly different tone. They presented pictures of themselves or others with their rifles or sitting with their quarry, sometimes mid-gralloch with sleeves rolled up, and they shared images of quarry being taken off the hill. They were honest depictions of the stalk, but I still found the images hard to look at. Some of the captions for these images were also respectful and insightful, whereas others just remarked on what a great day was had on the hill. I took no issue with what these stalkers and ghillies decided to share; after all, I had chosen to follow them, and I had wanted to get a sense of what a stalk entailed.

But I was curious as to why it appeared male stalkers seemed more comfortable sharing the less palatable aspects of stalking.

In 2018, the American Larysa Switlyk went viral after she shared images on Instagram from a hunting trip in Scotland. The images were no different in tone to those of the male stalkers I had seen, so what was the problem? Aside from her posing with a goat she'd shot on Islay, which is a little unusual, the outrage seemed to stem from her expression: she was smiling. People felt she was boasting and gloating in her captions rather than being respectful. It sparked a fierce outrage, and Scottish ministers even got involved, condemning the practice of wild-goat hunting as worse than deer stalking. Complaints were made to Police Scotland, and Switlyk was reported to the Procurator Fiscal for alleged firearms offences. No charges were ever brought against her, but as a result of the furore around the images, Switlyk received death threats, and there were calls to ban her from hunting in Scotland. Even now, there are still calls to ban her from social media. All this because a woman smiled with her legally obtained quarry. I could scroll through my timeline and bring up image after image of men doing the same thing, but it wouldn't spark the same outrage. Switlyk, as an American, comes from a different hunting culture, one where goat hunting is a more common sporting pursuit, but also where there are more women hunters. I can't help but wonder if this outrage was a manifestation of our internalised patriarchy, that we find it hard to accept the image of a woman as a hunter, dominating nature.

Women Warriors

In 2018, in the Andes, 9,000-year-old remains were discovered in a grave surrounded by a kit of sharpened stones and spear points. The remains were thought to be that of a male hunter because of this kit. If similar tools had been found with a known female, they might have been interpreted as scraping or cutting stones. However, analysis of the dental enamel revealed proteins that are associated with the biological sex of a female. As a result, this discovery contributed to a growing amount of evidence that challenged our understanding of ancient gender roles. The remains were thought to be the oldest that evidenced the existence of female big-game hunters in the Americas. Of course the evidence was fiercely scrutinised, and it was suggested that a male hunter must have buried his tools with the young female, perhaps in an act of grief or tribute. This theory highlighted an inherent gender bias, as the original ownership of the tools was only questioned after they were found to be with a female.

Back in 1878, in the global North, a Viking tomb was discovered in the town of Birka on the island of Björkö, Sweden, and amongst the graves were the remains of a great Viking warrior, along with weapons, a board for mapping out military strategy and two sacrificed horses. These objects and sacrifices led to the assumption that the remains were of a high-status male, maybe a military leader. Warriorhood was thought to be solely a masculine occupation, despite descriptions of female warriors throughout Norse lore.

The Birka warrior was presumed male for 139 years, until in 2017 a team from Uppsala University released the results of their DNA sequencing of the remains. The results revealed the biological sex of the warrior to be female. This result was strongly contested. Claims were made that the bones must have been mixed up with that of another grave during the excavation a century and a half earlier. Or perhaps mislabelled. Or the items found never belonged to the person in the grave.

Or perhaps the remains belonged to a transgender man, which led to a discussion around the misinterpretation of gender identity in past cultures and people. The team responsible for the discovery acknowledged that the term 'transgender' was a highly politicised Western concept and difficult to apply to people of the past, because our knowledge of the gender spectrum is limited to what we know now. It was, however, a reminder that we have a long history of conflating biological sex and gender identity. As the Birka warrior grave didn't contain any objects that would be typically associated with women, such as women's clothing or domestic items, it was assumed to be the grave of a high-status person or warrior, and therefore a man. Despite having been long accepted as a warrior burial site, the question of whether the site was even a tomb was soon under scrutiny, all because the Birka warrior was biologically female.

What the team had uncovered wasn't just a female warrior, or an awareness that other graves and remains are still subject to the same misidentification, but just how pervasive gender bias is in our understanding of the world and its history. This gender bias continues to permeate our understanding of the natural world. The terms 'human' and 'non-human' are often used to differentiate between our species and that of every other species in the world, with 'human' supposedly a genderless noun, but our experience isn't genderless, and neither is being human. The term 'human' is therefore understood by some, particularly ecofeminist thinkers, to be inherently patriarchal, because it's based on an understanding of ourselves and of the natural world that has predominantly been informed by the male experience, or more specifically that of the cis white male elite.

I have recently started exploring intersectional ecofeminism, and it offers a new perspective on how the impact of global economics, the redistribution of resources and the climate crisis disproportionately affect the lives of women across the world. Ecofeminism is a branch of feminism which argues broadly that the systems that oppress and destroy the natural and non-human world are the same systems that oppress and kill women. This stance is reinforced by a concept referred to as the 'master model'. In simplistic terms, the master model is a series of dualisms that require a subordinate other, such as a non-human entity, which then becomes appropriated into the culture of the dominant 'master'. Human and non-human, landowner and land, stalker and hind – the dominant master in these dualisms is associated with what are regarded as cis white male elite characteristics, such as rationality, civility, strength and domination, while the subordinate other is said to reflect characteristics such as irrationality, primitivism, weakness and submission. I find it interesting that these subordinate characteristics associated with the natural world are also associated with women, which ultimately 'others' women from the dominant experience. This othering becomes a system of oppression that can be used to disempower both women and non-human species. Ecofeminism challenges this system and the narrow patriarchal view of what is meant by 'human' experience.

Within Highland culture, these dualisms feel more overt. Nature and the non-human are continually made subordinate to the dominant human through land ownership, land management, species management, gamekeeping and even ecological restoration. Human needs or objectives are often prioritised over those of the environment, though relationships are often mutually reinforcing: the gamekeeper is dependent on the deer for their livelihood, and the deer are dependent on the gamekeeper for a hospitable habitat. The landowner is dependent on the gamekeeper to maintain the deer for the benefit of the sporting estate, and in turn the gamekeeper is dependent on the landowner for their livelihood. In male-dominated roles, such as landowner and gamekeeper, characteristics typically associated with being masculine, such as strength, logic and dominance, are prioritised over qualities associated with being feminine. In order to deconstruct these patriarchal systems of oppression, many ecofeminists argue that such roles and characteristics should be rejected through subversion, resistance and replacement.

I didn't realise it at the time, but I think this was why I felt apprehensive before the stalk. Not only was I willingly entering a male-dominated environment, but, in stepping into the dominant role within the dualism of stalker–hind, I would be expected to prioritise masculine characteristics over my own. I would have to be strong and domineering rather than sensitive and empathetic. I didn't have the tools or even know then that it might be possible to subvert or replace these masculine qualities, but afterwards, I began thinking about the ways in which we might interact with the land and non-human species without participating in the master model.

3

Glen Feshie

At the conference, a seed of doubt had been planted in my mind about the seemingly altruistic nature of rewilding. Almost two years later, after successive pandemic lockdowns and local restrictions, I was finally able to travel back to the Highlands and the Cairngorms National Park.

Once there, I found myself on a single-track road that led through a mix of old plantation forests and broadleaf woodland before eventually reaching Ballintean. On this particular June morning, it seemed as though the seasons had skipped summer and autumn altogether and dipped briefly back into winter. The sky was a flat grey and mist sat on the tops of the hills that lined the glen. This would be the backdrop for a morning in Glen Feshie with Peter Cairns, the executive director of Scotland: The Big Picture.

We met outside Ballintean Lodge, Cairns's other business. A large contemporary mountain lodge usually populated by international walking groups, it had understandably sat empty in recent months. Cairns strode up the track from his home to greet me. He was dressed in modern walking clothes and boots, had short fair hair, smiley expressive eyes and a wide grin. We greeted each other with an awkward elbow bump and got into his 4x4.

Peter had offered to take me into Glen Feshie and show me

some of the ecological changes he had witnessed first-hand over the 30 years that he'd lived there. The glen had become somewhat of a poster child for rewilding in Scotland, thanks in part to Cairns's advocacy work through Scotland: The Big Picture. Before and after pictures of Glen Feshie often did the rounds on social media, and one aspect of Cairns's work was helping the public to understand the role of rewilding in our landscapes. He often found himself at the forefront of the rewilding debate, navigating divisive land-management issues, listening to public opinion and perceptions and doggedly offering alternative perspectives. This was partly why I was drawn to speak to Peter: not only would he understand the dynamics at play, but he also had a part in influencing those dynamics.

We had only just left Ballintean when Peter started to share the Glen Feshie story, and, like any good storyteller, he began with the most contentious moment in the estate's recent history – when it was the site of Scotland's largest deer cull.

The now infamous cull took place in 2004, long before I had any interest or awareness of such events. The cull was said to have come about because the estate owner at the time had failed to reduce deer numbers and in turn failed to protect Glen Feshie's habitats and species. An intervention was organised by the then Deer Commission for Scotland to bring in hired guns to the estate and carry out a significant cull. It was estimated that in that year, the deer population was reduced by almost half, from around 1,500 to 800. The high numbers and nature of the cull led to opposition, disapproval and disagreements across Scotland's stalking and gamekeeping communities as well as local communities, animal-rights activists and the wider public.

As Peter explained the circumstances that led up to the cull, an image entered my head, that of deer being shot at indiscriminately from helicopters in a killing spree, a massacre akin to something from *Apocalypse Now.*

'That's a myth though, right?' I asked.

'Helicopters were used, but shooting from a helicopter's illegal in this country. They were used for extraction.'

Press headlines decried the 'massacre' alongside images of deer being extracted. Protests were held, and the whole event was seen as a PR nightmare that not only besmirched the work of stalkers and gamekeepers but plunged hunting further into disrepute.

So pervasive was the media's take on the Glen Feshie cull, that, nearly 20 years later, the more mythical aspects of the event had lodged themselves in my memory.

Since Anders Povlsen bought Glenfeshie Estate in 2006, strict culling targets had continually been met, not to avoid another culling intervention but to protect the estate's tree regeneration. I was about to observe the effects this had had on the glen.

*

We pulled over in a rough passing place near the old bridge and set off on foot along a track that runs parallel to the braided water courses of the River Feshie. At the lower end of the glen, four hills made for an epic foreground to our walk. The water level was low – there had been little rain or hill run-off in recent weeks – and the exposed riverbed was wide and gravelly. But the glen was vulnerable to flooding too: the Carnachuin Bridge was swept away in 2009, when the river had been in spate following heavy rain. It was hoped that the erosion around the river could be tackled naturally, in part with new riparian tree regeneration helping to stabilise areas of the bank.

Dead trees with large root plates lay in the riverbed. It was a sight you'd expect to see in a beaver habitat, but here, these trees had been placed in the river to provide shelter and shade for river species as well as to help slow the flow of the river. Timber for rebuilding the Carnachuin Bridge sat expectantly on the riverbank, waiting for planning issues to be resolved. The sun hadn't burnt away the morning cloud yet, and the grey stillness meant we were accompanied on our walk by one of Scotland's more abundant species, the midge. Fortunately I'm one of those annoying people that don't come up in bumps or hives even when bitten by them.

Peter continued to tell the Glen Feshie story, a tale of rewilding. He shared an example of a large-scale native woodland planting project on a neighbouring estate that he said had been inspired by the changes in Glen Feshie. The planting had been undertaken to improve biodiversity and sequester carbon, Peter told me with some enthusiasm. He saw this as clear evidence that landowners were changing, albeit slowly. He pointed out that there were estates that didn't necessarily like the changing trend in land management. But they were canny enough to know they needed to adapt to changes in economic trends, cultural values and consumer choices. At The Big Picture office, Peter told me, they received calls from people who didn't really like the idea of rewilding but knew they needed to get involved and even try to make money from it, through wild produce, experiential tourism, carbon initiatives, or even non-timber forest products. This showed that estates recognised the need to move away from a traditional model, which perhaps now had limited life in it, to new, innovative ways of managing their land, where the effects of climate breakdown and global biodiversity loss could be addressed alongside social and economic needs.

On one side of us was the river, lined with grasses and scrub. The other side of the track had more lush grasses, young trees and lots of blaeberries. We had barely begun our walk, and Peter was already tackling the big rural economic questions. I wanted to understand how it was that Peter found himself within Scotland's rewilding movement. Originally a photographer, he always wanted to tell environmental stories through his pictures, and he eventually became something of an environmental communicator. He found himself on the edge of conservation for a long time, before realising that approaches to conservation at the time weren't effective.

'Selecting individual species and habitats in isolation, wrapping cotton wool or a fence around them, whether metaphorical or real, wasn't working, because we had an accelerating decline in global biodiversity,' he said. I remembered Sir John Lister-Kaye of Aigas sharing this view at the Big Picture Conference. 'Then this thing came about that wasn't called rewilding, it was ecological restoration, and we moved from the idea of protection to recovery.'

This principle made sense to Peter, and he gradually became more involved in rewilding. He described it as being sucked into a vortex. I could relate to that: my obsession with land made me feel a little bit like Alice falling into the rabbit hole. There was no going back: I just had to follow, down, down, down, not past cupboards and empty jars of marmalade, but deeper and deeper into a tunnel of heated debates, environmental misconceptions and men in wax jackets with guns.

Peter's rabbit hole was Alladale. After Paul Lister purchased Alladale Estate in 2003, Peter was invited to document the work they were doing there, and he was involved in that process for a number of years. Peter even seemed to suggest that it was Lister who encouraged Povlsen to do something more positive with Glenfeshie after his purchase of the estate. Since then, the two landowners had apparently been engaged in a friendly rivalry. Those weren't Peter's exact words, but what he told me gave insight into the dynamics between Scotland's largest land-owner and Scotland's most controversial rewilder. I cringed ever so slightly at the idea that the improvement of Scotland's environment may stem mainly from a sense of competition between super-rich, powerful white men. Perhaps Peter read this in my expression as he offered some consolation: 'They both recognise they come from polluting industries and want to do their bit to give back. That's the motivation.'

The industries from which they made their money, fast fashion and flat-pack furniture, are still hugely polluting. They also disproportionately impact the lives of women of colour living in the global South. I couldn't help but feel a little greenwashing might be going on. I suppressed my burgeoning ecofeminist sensibilities, though. After all, Peter was just the messenger.

I told him that Lister was also my way into the rewilding movement. His intention to bring back the wolf, although fraught with controversy and risk, blew my mind and shifted my stance on the importance of protecting the environment: more vital was restoring it. Lister asked us to imagine a totally different Scotland, one I had never experienced, one that was a little bit dangerous and incredibly thrilling.

Peter explained that Lister's wolf idea had been instrumental in starting new conversations, fractious ones, yes, but it brought people round the table in discussion. The downside, however, was that, with Lister being dubbed the 'wolfman', the rewilding movement became synonymous with the species. Peter admitted that he was really tired of talking about wolves. He knew that when the media rang him, they wanted a sound bite about wolves that could be used to stir up tensions with farmers, for example. So he started to opt out of those conversations.

I remembered Peter's point about this in his opening provocation at The Big Picture conference in 2019. It had seemed as though shoulders dropped throughout the auditorium as tension was released: someone was willing to unapologetically address the wolf in the room.

The wolf was not the only challenge to the movement, though, Peter told me. 'Rewilding requires people to choose to do things differently. That might be in their gardens or allotments, or on 50,000 acres of land in the Highlands. At any scale, ecological blindness means we perceive the landscapes around us as beautiful and dramatic, but actually, in most cases they're ecologically knackered.'

He knew it was difficult to move people away from a comfortable and familiar mindset. 'We can reintroduce species and restore habitats, but it's about people changing their values and belief systems. You can't just click your fingers and tell people to think differently; you have to show them places like this and make it relevant to them.'

We'd been striding through Glen Feshie for fifteen minutes now, and I had been mostly staring at my feet. I stopped and invited Peter to draw our attention back to our surroundings. Without taking a beat, he jumped into a commentary on what surrounded us. Peter pointed out the blaeberries, heather and juniper, the latter of which he told me is rare in such abundance in Scotland. He gestured to the mosaic of woodland. We were surrounded by trees of different ages and species, with open glades and boggy ground, a variety of habitats. This brought him to a point he wanted to make about the current obsession with planting trees. We'd gone down a similar route before, which we'd regretted 40 years later. He believed we should be focusing on restoring a diverse range of habitats and carrying out tree planting in a way that is good for nature, climate and people. Creating habitat mosaics of forest and woodland, like at Glen Feshie, supports diversity of species, and even dead wood has huge environmental value.

Even I could see that this woodland was going through a process of natural regeneration, with its non-uniform spacing of saplings. Peter pointed out that this was possible here because there was already a seed source: it was much harder in areas where there might not be a tree within a 3-kilometre radius. It was also windy in the glen, and it had open fertile ground for tree growth. However, not all the regeneration was natural, and other areas on the estate were undergoing active afforestation.

We continued along the gravel path, and Peter pointed to some young rowans on the verge. The leaves had been nibbled at, most likely by a deer. It brought Peter to his next point. It's a misconception that there are no deer in Glen Feshie. There are, and they play a role in the ecology of the woodland and wider estate. It has been a case of balancing the grazing pressure to enable the vegetation to recover, and Peter confirmed that around 1,700 deer every year are still culled. This seemed like an extraordinary number and some feat. We stopped abruptly, and Peter showed me some more rowans, this time situated alongside some young aspens. He told me that in the presence of deer, these two species stand no chance. Their presence alone was evidence that the browsing pressure was low. But the presence of aspen was significant for another reason, too. Up until 20 years ago, Peter explained, it was rare to find aspen in Scotland, unless it was in a steep gorge that prevented browsing species from reaching it.

There was a lot of information to take in, but I really appreciated the opportunity to observe such positive changes in the glen. We started walking again, and the aspens prompted Peter to remember another moment that changed his mindset. He recalled being at an event around the time of the Knapdale beaver trials, when Insh Marshes was being considered as another potential beaver trial site. A concern was raised by conservationists regarding the potential impact on aspen, which beavers love. It became apparent that they couldn't have aspen if there were beavers, though they couldn't have beavers unless there was aspen. The conversation was reduced to having one or the other, and this left Peter perplexed. Single-species management was an issue he witnessed time and time again in conservation, even though this kind of siloed thinking was perhaps more commonly associated with sporting estates and the management of deer or grouse. In the end, he said, 'It's nothing to do with wood ants, or beavers, or wolves: it's people.'

It was a strange paradox he had highlighted: the aim of rewilding was to create self-willed habitats free of human inter-vention, but habitats ultimately needed human intervention to allow for ecological restoration, such as with the deer cull. I'd heard Peter saying that rewilding was 90 per cent about people. I had taken this as reassuring, as I'd assumed he meant it was about radical localism and community support, but in this context he seemed to mean something quite different.

I asked Peter if he thought there was a connection between rewilding and the feeling of ecological grief that people experi-ence. Unwavering in his role as a consummate environmental communicator, Peter recalled an Aldo Leopold quote: 'One of the penalties of an ecological education is that one lives alone in a world of wounds.' The words resonated.

As a photographer, Peter was very familiar with looking at Scottish landscapes, seeing ecological degradation and feeling the burden of that knowledge. I could relate to how devastating it would be to realise that the landscapes you were photographing, that you once understood as 'epic' or 'wild', were in fact degraded.

Peter admitted that the deeper he dug into this story of ecological destruction, the more depressing it became.

'In my mind I had to flip that, say we are where we are. Whoever's fault it was, it's history. We've now got challenges relevant to the 21st century. How can we move forward? Because there's no point looking back. It's not a question of what Scotland *should* look like, but what Scotland *could* look like, and that can be a country with a greater abundance of diversity of life. And that life absolutely includes human life.'

Peter felt strongly about not looking to the past. He found it tough, though, when people were intoxicated by rewilding or saw it as hope, as a passport to a bright future.

His train of thought was abruptly derailed as he spotted what seemed to be pine marten scat on the path. We both leaned over the dark coiled squiggle. Pine marten scat can be differentiated from fox poo by scent, but neither of us offered to investigate further to confirm.

Peter saw the increased interest and involvement in regeneration at Glen Feshie and other sites as a positive sign, though there were still plenty of heated debates going on in the chat sections of the rewilding webinars he had been involved with over the past year or so.

I suggested it might be easier to advocate for something you could already see happening around you. I think this annoyed Peter, or at least he had had this suggestion levelled at him before, because he was quick with an informed rebuttal: 'Glen Feshie is landscape-scale rewilding, but rewilding in our book is anything that moves us away from de-wilding. That's not just a physical thing; it's spiritual and emotional. It can even be done on your back doorstep.'

We approached the bottom of the glen, and the hills ganged up in front of us. We paused on the ecotone, a meeting-point of two habitats – in this case, the regenerated woodland and open grasslands. The blaeberry bushes gradually thinned away, and a mature tree stood in isolation ahead of us, the remnant of a much older woodland. I wondered whether this area was once a wooded glen, or, a century ago, an open area or hilltop managed for deer. As if echoing the past century, three white ponies browsed the grasslands. At one time, the retired stalking ponies would have assisted in carrying quarry off the hill or out the glen. The ponies were now used for luxury pony picnics, an activity offered to guests who stayed with Wildland at Glenfeshie or Killiehuntly estates. It wasn't just the upmarket experience, Peter told me, that was the appeal of these picnics; it was also the expertise of the keepers, and their storytelling.

'Hearing those voices and stories can fundamentally change someone's perspective,' he told me.

'But the price of that experience is prohibitive to the major-ity of people. There's a community of people in this area that can't afford to experience that.' I held my breath, unsure how Peter would take my remark.

'It's a legitimate argument, but there are other experiences with other companies that are accessible,' he fired back. This was obviously not the first time this had been put to him either. He countered again with examples of rewilding projects happening in urban areas. But I was interested in the communities in the Highlands who didn't have access to these quintessential luxury experiences. It was arguably selling a romanticised version of Highland culture which few locals would ever experience. I certainly never had. I didn't say this to Peter.

At this point, we turned back and retraced our steps along the glen. 'The democracy of rewilding has a long way to go,' said

Peter. 'There's no doubt. It's why we instigated the Northwoods Rewilding Network, to make the movement accessible to people who aren't Povlsen, Rausing or Lister. We do have to broaden its doors though, to let more people through. We're not where we need to be, and actions are being taken.'

During the drive into the glen, Peter had already mentioned that concerns had been raised about rewilding in terms of neocolonialism. Having touched upon the issue of accessibility, this seemed as good a moment as any to bring it up again.

'Why do you think people accuse the movement of being neocolonial?' I asked.

'Most people, rightly or wrongly, perceive rewilding as being done to them,' Peter said. 'It's not being done with them, it's being done *for* them by outsiders. Outsiders might be middle-class English academics or the government, or members of the establishment dictating rural land use.'

He recognised that those people felt voiceless and powerless, and that this new notion of rewilding challenged their belief systems. I wondered exactly what belief systems he might be referring to.

'My job is to turn rewilding from a perceived threat into an actual opportunity, an opportunity for a richer landscape, for climate mitigation but, critically, for young people.'

'Can you see, though,' I said, 'that the people both leading the rewilding movement and also managing the land are typically white, privileged men? They are perhaps on a different mission, but they look the same as colonial oppressors.'

To his credit, Peter agreed emphatically. 'Yes, although I would caveat that by saying that the motivation is different. This is not wealth dictating land use, this is societal threats dictating land use. There's a big difference between the industrial Victorians displacing people and rewilding that genuinely seeks to mitigate three existential emergencies.' Namely, biodiversity loss, climate change and rural decline.

Peter was aware of his language here, and he knew that using the term 'decline' was divisive. These were difficult and sensitive issues to talk about, and Peter was ultimately an advocate and communicator. He wasn't making decisions on the ground in places like Glen Feshie, but he definitely influenced the discourse around rewilding. I was reassured, in a sense, that he could and did acknowledge these issues. I was starting to get a much deeper understanding of the movement, beginning to see the wood *and* the trees.

I pushed further. 'It doesn't feel like it's a grassroots movement: it's top-down rather than bottom-up.' This was the difficulty I had with the rewilding movement in its current form, I explained. I couldn't escape that or easily put it aside, because in the Highlands we had a historically difficult relationship with the landowner–tenant dualism. Perhaps rewilding couldn't fix that, and maybe it wasn't its job to subvert that dualism. I realised that my expectations of rewilding were perhaps unrealistic.

We were still walking back to the 4x4, and I had been in my head the whole time, trying to listen and process the conversation. I wasn't looking up anymore to take in the glen. Perhaps if I had been on a luxury pony picnic I could have been more focused on the land, been more present, but I was in the company of a great storyteller, and it was testament to the depth of our conversation that I was not continually distracted by micro species or trying to spot deer or birds of prey.

I asked Peter for his thoughts on community stalking, and I was surprised to learn that Wildland had considered doing this as part of their social agenda, not out of benevolence but for reasons of social justice. He told me other places were also considering community stalks and assured me that democratising access to rewilding and land practices was on the agenda, though he did mention one particular landowner's refusal to do it, because, as he put it, they were a snob.

Before we returned to Ballintean, I wanted to talk to Peter about another topic in which I'd become increasingly interested: Gaelic. *Tha mi ag ionnsachdh Gàidhlig* – just on Duolingo, but still. I asked him for his thoughts on the role of Gaelic in rewilding. He referred to the work of Trees for Life and the new centre at Dundreggan that was being built. As well as ecological restoration, the centre's objectives included cultural revitalisation through Gaelic. I'd been fortunate enough, before meeting Peter, to have spoken to some of the women that had led that project, and I knew that a tremendous amount of work had gone into understanding the Gaelic history of place names, songs and poems from around Dundreggan and Glen Moriston. Gaelic offers us a unique insight into how land was understood and used by our ancestors. Although Peter absolutely saw a role for Gaelic, he felt some trepidation about its association with the past or using it to turn the clock back to recreate a utopian wilderness. Even if I didn't agree, I could appreciate what he was saying. Earlier in our walk, he had referred to the Ruighe Aiteachain bothy in the glen, telling me that the name meant 'glen of juniper'. He worried that this historical reference to juniper could provoke the kind of siloed thinking that he was so against, with management of that glen becoming species-specific and rewilded in favour of juniper. Peter knew that for some it was the 're' of rewilding that was objectionable, as it suggested a desire to go back in time. 'Equally,' he said, 'words like regeneration and revitalisation simply imply "again"; we're going again.'

'Redistribute,' I cheekily threw in.

'Redistribute, yeah. It's not always about going back, it's about reinvention, re-energising.'

For others like myself, it was the 'wilding' bit of rewilding that didn't sit well. The legacy of mass depopulation of the Highlands made me suspicious of anything that appeared to erase, consciously or unconsciously, any more of our social and cultural history. There was another side of me, however, that still enjoyed the bold ambition that the term rewilding inspired.

Peter could see the value in concepts such as shifting baselines and even deep time, but he reiterated that he was more future-focused. 'They're useful tools, but right here, right now, if we don't get off our backsides and do something, your children, your children's children, are going to be facing a world that's difficult to live in.'

Our conversation had reached a topic that I found emotionally very difficult: the future. Peter didn't know it, but a passing remark about how we'd be engaged in wars over water in the future almost sent me head first into existential crisis. My insides hardened as if turning to stone, and I could only respond to Peter with a series of sighs and stammers.

'The more urgent the problem becomes, the bigger the scale of change we need,' he continued.

I took a deep breath to try to relieve the grip of dread. I blurted out something about Cairngorms Connect's 200-year vision and how I couldn't envision a world 200 years from now. Peter misinterpreted what I was trying to say.

'As a species, we need to think long term. We need to think beyond ourselves and our immediate family. We can't talk about population: it's an uncomfortable conversation, it's culturally and politically sensitive; but we do determine how many deer are appropriate.'

My ears pricked at this remark and what it might have

alluded to. The petrification moved up into my diaphragm and forced out a confession of sorts.

'I can't imagine there even being generations in the future.'

Peter's demeanour subtly shifted. For a moment the environmental communicator looked concerned. He started with a response but stuttered before regaining composure.

'But what that does . . . I know it's not a conclusion that you've set out to achieve . . . but it could paralyse you into inaction.'

'I'm trying to undo that.'

'You've got to, you've got to. Rewilding does offer hope, or at least a journey to something better, and we need to see that.'

4

Encounters

Abandoned

'Drop your bag. We need to go up the lane.'

'Why?' a preteen me asked my mum.

'Just do it.'

Hearing the urgency in her voice, I quickly threw my school bag in my bedroom and met her outside our front door.

'What's going on?'

'Wait 'til you see.' The urgency in her voice had a hint of disquiet.

We speedily walked the few hundred yards up the lane to our neighbour's home. It wasn't unusual for us to visit our neighbour together. Mum would usually go in for a catch up while I played on the swing in the back garden, surreptitiously picked fruit from the greenhouse or checked to see whether the local hedgehog had eaten any food from the saucer left out for it.

We walked through the gate and up to the front door. Mum gently tapped the large brass lion-head knocker.

'You'll need to be very quiet,' she told me.

I was always very quiet, so this piqued my curiosity.

We tentatively entered the bungalow. The dog was not around to conduct its usual terrifying greeting ritual. We opened the door into the living room, and saw our neighbour

48

standing there, smiling at me. The room was very quiet. All I could hear were the gears and the swinging pendulum of the clock in the kitchen next door.

'Jenna,' she said. 'Look here.' She pointed to the armchair.

I didn't notice it at first, as it was almost indistinguishable from the swirly pattern and autumnal browns of the uphol-stery. But then I saw: nestled into the cushions was a very small fawn. It was sitting with its disproportionately long front legs tucked under the sides of its chest. Its large ears stuck out from the sides of its head, and its little wet nose sniffed the air. Dark eyes peeped out from underneath its long eyelashes. Its breath-ing was fast. I stood staring at it. Careful not to move quickly, I turned to look at my neighbour, unable to hide a look of sheer disbelief.

'We found it on the golf course. It's been abandoned by its mother.'

I had seen deer in the neighbouring golf course during many of my clandestine tree-climbing visits there, but never a fawn.

I felt something tighten in the pit of my stomach. Why had such a young fawn been abandoned by its mother? But more importantly, why had my neighbours brought it here? Like most children, I had been told from a young age that you should never touch a baby animal. Doing so could dramatically reduce its chances of survival. But I didn't say this. I could see by my mother's expression that she was also unsettled.

I watched the fawn. It sat stock-still, paralysed by the alien environment.

'The SSPCA will be coming shortly. Would you like to hold it?' my neighbour asked.

Before I could reply, she moved to the armchair and scooped up the fawn. She nodded at the seat, signalling for me to sit down.

I know I shouldn't have, but I did. She gently placed the fawn on my lap. It was warm with a little bit of weight to it. I looked down at the white dappled markings on its back and its thin velvety ears, its fragile legs splayed out. It didn't try to move or get away; it just accepted what was happening. I kept my arms at my sides and didn't pet it.

It was an extraordinary thing to experience, but the circumstances didn't feel good. It was emotional, almost sorrowful. The actions of my neighbour meant that the fawn's life had changed irrevocably. What was going to happen to it? I wondered. It would surely never see its mother again. The heavy stone-like feeling in my gut spread as I recalled the Disney movie *Bambi*.

Somebody took out a camera.

'Smile.'

I let a small smile grow. My eyes didn't betray my concern.

The camera flashed, and I felt a little jolt of panic from my lap.

'Right, let's go,' announced my mum.

The little fawn was quickly but carefully lifted off me. It was a relief to be leaving, but I wanted to know what would happen next. As I was directed out the door, I caught a final glimpse of the animal, gathered up in my neighbour's arms like a bundle of twigs. Silent.

I never heard about the fawn again, and I don't remember asking about it either. I kept the photo that was taken that day, and whenever I looked at it, those conflicted feelings came back. I knew even then, as I held the fawn, that it hadn't been abandoned. It had been accidentally taken. My neighbours were unaware that fawns were often left for hours at a time by their mothers. Even if we'd told them at the time, though, it would have been too late; the damage had already been done.

The Museum

A couple of years after that, we moved to the outskirts of Inverness. There was no public transport in the area, and to get to town I had to either walk the mile and a half to the nearest bus stop or rely on my parents. On weekends, before I was old enough to work, I'd sometimes get dropped off at the top of Stephen's Brae or the Raining Steps and wander down to the high street. I'd usually venture in on my own, with instructions to be outside the town hall at a certain time to be picked up. Unlike most teenagers, I rarely went into town to buy clothes or make-up. I would pass the other teenagers congregated outside Burger King and head away from the shopping centre. The reverberations of the busker's guitar would grow louder down the lane near Woolworths. More groups of teenagers, this time congregated outside McDonald's. I'd cross the road at the Town House, pass its gothic entrance and turn up the brae to possibly one of the most inconspicuous Highland cultural institutions at the time, the Inverness Museum and Gallery. I would walk determinedly into the foyer, past the visitor desk, which was guarded by Felicity the taxidermied puma, and up the stairs. I wasn't there for the cafe or the art gallery; there was only one collection that interested me. I didn't know its official name, but I referred to it as the room with the animals.

It was low-ceilinged, grey and gloomy, with a small window in the far corner. And it was filled with glass display cases of all shapes and sizes, each with their own different model habitat and a collection of taxidermied animals specific to the British Isles or the Highlands. There was a wildcat stretching up a tree trunk, possibly reaching towards a red squirrel or a pine marten. A displaying male capercaillie in a woodland scene. Various small rodents situated in what was supposed to be a domestic setting. A tiny taxidermied pipistrelle suspended between two fake brick walls.

My two favourites were the fox and the badger. Both of them sat free of a display case; both looked tired. I could never resist giving the badger and the fox a very gentle pat, and the fur around their eyes, head and snouts was missing from years of being touched by visitors like me. I stood in front of them, taking in the different textures and colourings of the fur on their stiff, inanimate bodies, and they sat on the carpet-tiled floor staring blankly past me as if turned to stone. I took in the characteristics of each species. Their size, their proportions. The European badger with its pointed claws and leathery nose. The red fox with its sharp features and wiry tail. It was macabre, but not distressing. Unlike with the live fawn, my proximity couldn't scare the animals. Their paralysis wasn't fear, just death.

Satisfied with the fox and the badger, I'd wander from case to case, absorbed in each display and looking for any species I hadn't noticed before, hidden in the scenic lichen moss and grasses, but the displays rarely changed, if ever. This was calming. These little habitats frozen in time. Little worlds.

The ancient peoples collection occupied the other half of the room. These cabinets didn't have the same atmospheric, otherworldly quality of the taxidermy displays. They were white and sterile and contained old beads, copper brooches, bracelets, gnarly belts, arrowheads. In the centre of the collection was a big table-top display in a glass case. It might have been a model of a settlement, maybe Pictish. It's only really the unpalatable smell I remember now, like old chocolate cereal mixed with clay.

From the window, I could see the clock on Bridge Street and know when it was time to leave. I would quickly make my way out through the ancient peoples collection and past the enormous taxidermied rutting stag that stood alone on a white rostra at the entrance to the room, leaning slightly to the right as if its sparring partner had vanished mid blow. I never remembered to spend time with this piece, perhaps because it wasn't in the collection itself, or perhaps because it stood out of context, with no suggestion of its natural environment. It was a rutting gatekeeper, safeguarding the liminal space between the bright upper foyer of the world of the living and the dark realm of taxidermy and ancient people.

*

In 2017, I went back to the museum for the first time since I'd left Inverness to go to university. I had come up to see Edwin Landseer's *The Monarch of the Glen*. Earlier that year, the National Galleries of Scotland had acquisitioned the painting, bringing it into public hands for the first time, and, to mark the occasion, it toured four Scottish galleries, including Inverness Museum and Gallery. The subject of the painting is a twelve-point or 'royal' stag with an epic, misty backdrop of mountains and a heavy, threatening sky. The stag shows an exposed right flank, the most vulnerable to a hunter's aim, and it gazes majestically, or perhaps attentively, out to the left, past the viewer, perhaps alerted to another presence on the hill. I'd only ever seen the painting in print before – on postcards, whisky bottles, mugs, cushions, keyrings and, of course, biscuit tins – and I was excited to see in person the original of one of the most iconic images associated with Scotland, and specifically the Highlands.

Originally commissioned in 1849 for the refreshment room in the House of Lords, the painting was completed around the time of the purchase of the Balmoral Estate by Queen Victoria and Prince Albert in 1852. This was a period when deer stalking attracted the wealthy to the Highlands, and Landseer's work was popular.

Although Landseer himself enjoyed shooting in Scotland, at the time the painting was bought by the National Galleries of Scotland, a tabloid newspaper claimed that the stag in *The Monarch of the Glen* was in fact not Scottish but one from a herd in Cambridgeshire, where Landseer was known to paint. The translocation of an English deer to the Scottish Highlands mirrored what was happening in deer management on sporting estates in that era. Typically for the purpose of stocking, restocking or improving the 'bloodstock' on an estate, larger deer would be moved from England to the Highland estates, in the belief that their future offspring would benefit from their genetics.

*

Just like in previous years, I was dropped off at one end of the high street and made my way over to the other. The busker had vanished now, and Woolworths was long gone. The museum had been renovated since my last visit, too. For the first time, I went into the gallery space, and I was greeted by the work *After, After, After, After The Monarch of the Glen: Real Life is Dead* by Scottish artist Ross Sinclair. The work had been commissioned as a response to Landseer's painting. The room was half filled with items that had been given a Scottish kitsch makeover. Neon signs proclaimed things like 'We ♥ Edwin Landseer' and 'We ♥ Bannockburn'. The top half of a Land Rover adorned with its own set of trophy antlers sat in the middle of the installation, as if submerged in a bog. A couple of laminated posters were positioned side by side on the wall, one with 'real life' and the other with 'land seer' written on. Reading the text horizontally across the posters, it became 'real land' and 'life seer'.

The pinks, yellows, blues and reds of the neon evoked a feeling of an underground bar or club or perhaps the vaults beneath George IV bridge in Edinburgh. After the sensory explosion of Sinclair's work and the questions it raised about our Scottish cultural identity, I turned to see *The Monarch of the Glen*, the only painting on an otherwise blank white wall at the far end of the room. A single light with a cool wash focused on it from the lighting track above. The painting was much, much smaller than I'd imagined. I expected the stag to tower over me from its gilt-edged frame. But it didn't. It was a modest size, just over a metre and a half in width and height, almost a square. I walked over to it. I was the only one in the gallery. Finally, the majestic stag and I stood almost eye to eye. The smoky blue hues of the mountain mist in the background gave the painting a tranquil quality. It may be 170-odd years old, but much of the Highlands still looks the same as it did then. I wondered what other people thought about when they looked at the painting. Did conservationists note the treeless uplands and scrub at the stag's feet? Did stalkers subconsciously assess the condition of the creature to determine whether it was to be culled that year? Did the landowner see in the stag the value it might bring to an estate?

I reflected on my own attitude towards the painting. It was both synonymous with the Highlands and yet reflected little of my lived experience. At the time, I felt that this kind of Highland romanticism was impeding contemporary land-management issues. I believed that deer were vermin, to be controlled and culled.

The Pass

We used to drive down the A9 from Inverness to visit family in the Central Belt a few times a year. Shell-suited and strapped in, we'd settle down for a journey which always felt like eight hours but in reality was only three or so. I'd get the passenger side of the backseat by default because my brother preferred, for whatever reason, to sit behind the driver. The journey was made bearable by my pink Sony Walkman. I'd load it up with whatever cassette my brother wasn't intending to listen to, pop on my adjustable headphones with orange foam ear cushions, lean my head back and let the road trip wash over me as the country whizzed past.

There were four specific landmarks that I would look out for. The first was the Slochd Summit mimetolith, a formation on the rock face that resembled a soldier in a helmet. Once you knew what to look for, you could easily spot it from any direction. Second was a wooden treehouse at the edge of a pine plantation before the turn-off for Carrbridge. I watched enviously as we passed, thinking how much I'd like to sit in it. I wonder now if it was a hunting blind, in fact, and not a tree-house. The third was my second cousin's house at Kingussie, which we could see from the A9. We'd all wave as we passed, pretending they could see us. The fourth landmark marked the gateway between the highlands and the lowlands for me. Drumochter Pass. It was the last stronghold of the Munros along the A9 before the landscape gradually flattened into agricultural land.

In winter the peaks would be covered in brilliant white snow, with drifts threatening to close the A9 entirely. In autumn, with the turn of the heather, the hills were a vibrant purple. In spring, the snow-melt cascaded off the slopes. But most excitingly, and in any season, the hillsides would be covered with deer. In early winter they could be found on the lower ground around the River Spey, on the Balsporran side of the pass. In summer, they would be on the high tops on the opposite side of the pass.

I'd press my nose to the car window once we'd passed the distillery at Dalwhinnie and look to the hillsides and summits. At speed, they looked a bit like a Magic Eye stereogram, which were hugely popular at the time. I would widen my focus and try to spot any out-of-the-ordinary colours or shapes in my peripheral vision. A raised head, the white flash of a tail, a shake of an antler, or a scatter of russet-coloured bodies. There was nothing more satisfying than spotting a herd grazing.

'Deer!' I'd gleefully announce once I'd spotted them. I was so good at finding deer at the pass that I began to believe I had some sort of gift for it. In reality, I was probably the only one looking. I'd check both sides of the pass as we neared the tree plantation around the large white lodge on the left then passed Balsporran on the right. Once we hit Glen Garry, I would stop looking. On the return journey, the pass would always bring a sense of comfort, a feeling of finally being home. Even years later, I'd still look for a herd on the tops and the hillsides. I watched the area change over the years. With every trip south and north, new tracks emerged over the peaty hummocks and up to the scree tops. Then came the Beauly-Denny powerline and larger laybys on the A9, allowing walkers and tourists safer access to the hills.

I always wanted to explore Drumochter Pass, climb the Munros, walk to Loch Garry and along Loch Ericht, but I never did. I was always too eager to get home. Having explored much of Scotland, I knew that Drumochter Pass wasn't really the most scenic of landscapes that Scotland had to offer. The Three Sisters, Torridon and the Cuillin trump the pass several times over for their scenic quality. But I still felt a connection to Drumochter, rooted in my childhood, in my relationship to deer, to landscape. And, later, I would learn that my links to Drumochter were even stronger than I realised.

The Shooting Lodge

A rumour had been doing the rounds within the wider family for years. Some family members believed that we had an ancestral connection with the 1st Duke and Duchess of Sutherland, who were responsible for the Highland Clearances. Feeling conflicted and intrigued in equal measure, I started looking into it on the National Archives of Scotland's online database, ScotlandsPeople. I quickly jumped a few generations and followed a maternal line back decades, and eventually centuries, up the east coast of Scotland, past Sutherland to Thurso, then on to the Orkneys and into the seventeeth century. I found what I thought could be the source of the rumours, but it would require professional assistance to know for sure. During the search I accumulated files full of documents: census records, birth certificates, death certificates, military service records, marriage certificates and even the odd photograph. I used two other genealogical search engines to corroborate the connections I'd made and to help me build a user-friendly family tree. I never strayed far from the individuals that were leading me back along a particular branch.

It wasn't until a couple of years later that I reopened the folder on my computer. I'd become much more interested in land ownership and wanted to understand the impact of the Clearances on my ancestors. I was interested in why my family moved from the north Highlands to Newtonmore and eventually gained a croft. I looked back over the records I'd collated in previous years, curious as to what they could tell me now. I was hoping to make a list of places where my family had lived and check it against any Clearance records. I started in Newtonmore with my grandfather's birth certificate. Then back a generation with my great-grandfather, whom I'd never met, to Cromdale, heading northwards. I found out he was a gamekeeper – interesting; I'd always assumed he was a crofter. A century back now to my great-great-grandfather. He was registered in the parish of Laggan, further south again. I hastily looked through the column and rows for easily legible text. *Occupation: Gamekeeper.* Two generations of gamekeepers in the family. Then, *Name of House.* I dragged my finger down the column until I reached his name. Written in the adjacent box, in a black scrawl on the sepia page was *Shooting Lodge.* I'd never heard of anyone in the family living in a shooting lodge. I moved back up the column to find out exactly where in the Laggan parish they were. In the top box of the column was the estate name: *Drumochter.*

I gasped in disbelief and checked it again. But I had read it correctly: according to the census, my great-great-grandfather and his family had lived in the Drumochter shooting lodge.

I quickly opened a map app on my phone and typed the address into the search bar. A red pin dropped, and I zoomed in. The pin had landed beside the A9 on the large white lodge near Balsporran. It couldn't be. I looked it up on a digital OS map. Same result. I went to the old 1970s map of Kingussie and Newtonmore that we have framed in the hall. I followed the A9 with my fingertip and stopped just shy of Balsporran. *Lodge.*

Back at my computer, I followed my great-great-grandfather through the census. In 1881, he was an unmarried labourer living near Fort William. By 1891, he had arrived at the lodge and was a gamekeeper. The 1911 census recorded that the family was still in the shooting lodge, with two more sons working as gamekeepers. For at least 30 years, my family had lived and worked on the Drumochter estate as gamekeepers and ghillies. I sat back in my chair, delighted by the revelations.

Drumochter Hills

I wondered now whether my complicated relationship with the concept of landownership was informed by more than my identity as a Highlander – had I also somehow inherited a wariness, or perhaps a curiosity, towards estate life? My knowledge of estates was limited to the performative pastiches of the Victorian era that I would occasionally glimpse at Highland tourist attractions or on the telly. Tweed, plus fours, wax jackets, rifles, dogs, and absentee landowners. The hierarchical social structures of estates had never sat comfortably with me. Some historians argue that the establishment of sporting estates centuries ago by the landed gentry was an attempt to bring modernity to the rural Highlands, to bring order to a supposedly backwards and rebellious region. That dualism, in which Highlanders were the subordinate other, left me feeling peeved.

From the outside, Drumochter looked like a traditional sporting estate, with large areas of moor that had been burned to maintain a habitat for grouse and livestock-grazing. Over the years, I'd occasionally spotted a shooting party whilst passing on the A9, but I had seen little else. I was curious about what it meant for Drumochter to be within the boundary of the Cairngorms National Park but not a participant of Cairngorms Connect. And did the neighbouring landowners influence or irk each other?

The installation of the Beauly–Denny powerline, a 137-mile network of 615 mega pylons, was one of the biggest changes I witnessed when I travelled up and down this stretch of A9. From Beauly, it cut a path down to Fort Augustus through Glen Moriston, just a few miles south of Dundreggan. From there it ran southeast towards Ardverikie and on to Dalwhinnie, eventually meeting up with Drumochter. The need for the powerline was first identified around 2003: a new transmission line with increased capacity was needed to transfer the energy generated from renewables to the national grid. It was considered a hugely important piece of infrastructure allowing Scotland to compete in the renewable energy market. The first opposition community group, Stirling Before Pylons, was founded in late 2004. In 2006, three local authorities opposed the proposal with the Highlands and Islands, asking for further evidence regarding potential health concerns. Shortly after, Scottish ministers requested a public inquiry, followed by more opposing community groups including the Beauly–Denny Landscape Group. In 2009, the Cairngorms National Park Authority objected to the erection of the Scottish and Southern Electricity Networks' mega pylons on the northern hills of Drumochter on the grounds that the proposal came into conflict with their aims as a national park. They created their own campaign, humorously called Cairngorms Revolt Against Pylons, or CRAP, for short.

In 2010, following the longest ever public inquiry in Scotland, the Scottish ministers granted consent to the project, with pre-construction work beginning at the end of that year. In total, the Beauly–Denny powerline development was met with nearly 20,000 objections.

I remember feeling taken aback that mega pylons were being constructed in Drumochter. Each trip on the A9 revealed a new pylon, a new scar on the landscape, and I asked myself what impact the powerline would have on the deer. I actually knew very little about Drumochter's biodiversity and decided to find out more.

I found a digitised map of Drumochter from the 1900s, and on it, of course, was the shooting lodge. There was obviously no A9 then, nor mega pylons, but the Highland railway and

General Wade's road were both recorded. Thinking back to my conversation with Peter and how Gaelic was sometimes used as a tool in rewilding, I wrote a list of all the Gaelic names for landmarks in the area, curious as to what these toponyms might reveal. I came to understand some basic meanings: *allt* means burn; *coire*, corrie; *creagan*, small rock, and so on. I came across a familiar word, although I didn't know its meaning: *cailleach*. I assumed it had something to do with women or girls. Cailleach Coire Chùirn. My Gaelic wasn't good enough to decipher what it meant. Nearby was a track that took a route high above the corrie along to A' Bhuidheanach. I checked a contemporary OS map, and the track still existed; perhaps I could walk it.

Corrour and Drumochter were separated by only one estate, Ben Alder. It was strange to realise just how close and interconnected these landscapes really were. I imagined herds of stags and hinds wandering across the tops of Drumochter, through Ben Alder's glens and into Corrour. I realised I had no sense of whether Scotland's deer population had migratory routes, what their range might be and whether there were established patterns to their movements.

Eager to know more about the biodiversity of Drumochter, I searched Scotland's Environment Map. It revealed that the main characteristic of the Drumochter Hills are their high-altitude plateaus. These, combined with abundant heather, make the area an ideal breeding site for merlins and dotterel, and as a result, it has been designated a Special Protection Area since 1997.

Merlins are the UK's smallest falcon, only a little bit bigger than a blackbird. They nest on the ground, usually in upland habitats, and are on the UK conservation Red list, meaning they are most in need of protection. The last available public

NatureScot assessment of the area in 2004 recorded it as 'unfavourable' for this species, with burning and overgrazing listed as the most prevalent negative pressures. I listened to the merlin's call on the RSPB website. It had a repeating long screech that went slightly up in pitch at the end of the call, sometimes increasing in intensity. I would definitely have mistaken it for a coastal bird.

Dotterels are part of the plover family and breed on the plateaus of Scottish mountains. They scrape out a little groove in the ground to create a shallow nest, and the clutch is vulnerable to accidental damage. Dotterels are also on the UK's Red list, and the latest NatureScot assessment notes that their numbers are declining on the hills, again due to overgrazing and trampling from deer and livestock. I was reminded of Lynbreck Croft and its approach to working with the land and not in conflict with it, avoiding the types of land- and habitat-management practices that could impact negatively on other species.

Drumochter is also a designated Special Area of Conservation for its habitats, characterised as dry heaths, alpine, boreal heaths, scrub, grasslands and blanket bogs. The Joint Nature Conservation Committee went into some detail about the species found on the Drumochter Hills. The negative pressures on these habitats were again described as burning, overgrazing by deer and trampling. The condition assessment remained unfavourable and unchanged.

The last designation of Drumochter was as a Site of Special Scientific Interest (SSSI) for its ground-nesting birds and montane species. The statement gave an account of why the Drumochter Hills area is of national importance: its high-altitude plateaus are host to extensive arctic-alpine species. This is particularly significant because they are remnants believed to have survived the last glaciation. Other notable species include the rare blue heath or *Phyllodoce caerulea*, which has been recorded on the hills as recently as 2020. The only other place in Scotland that was known to have blue heath was Ben Alder.

With some trepidation, partly because I could sense some confronting truths were coming my way, I continued to read the SSSI statement. Having never walked the hills and only travelled the pass by car, it was impossible to get a sense of the multitude of species that existed on the Drumochter Hills beyond sheep, deer, cattle and heather, lots and lots of heather. It seemed I had fallen for one of the biggest misconceptions going, that any Scottish landscape devoid of trees and covered in heather was a bleak monoculture. I believed the same about blanket bog before I came to realise the biodiversity that our peatlands could support, as well as how effective it was at sequestering carbon. The SSSI statement continued with lists of species that have been found on the Drumochter Hills and their importance: the nationally scarce downy willow or *Salix lapponum*, and *Ceraticum alpimun*, *Saxifraga nivalis*, *Carex rupestris*, *Athyrium distentifolium*. A series of Latin names that were totally meaningless to me. Then onto birds: ptarmigan, snow bunting, golden eagle, greenshank and wigeon.

The advice for management of the hills outlined how the process of burning heather had reduced the amount of taller heather available as a breeding habitat for merlins. It had impacted the natural regeneration of trees and scrub, which, combined with overgrazing from livestock and deer, meant the habitat would take a long time to recover. It was noted that best practice guidance hadn't always been followed: the burning had in the past encroached on steeper slopes and ridges, which caused erosion, making breeding grounds more vulnerable.

Sections of the northern hills of Drumochter were known to have a high density of deer: recent counts showed one area in particular had more than 100 per square kilometre, which, given culling targets, was almost unbelievable. Some of the southern Drumochter hills were surrounded by areas with densities of between 14 and 61 per square kilometre. Data around deer–vehicle collisions showed regular incidents each year on the A9 throughout the pass. It was a sobering reminder that the deer cull could reduce not only overgrazing but also the likelihood of life-threatening road collisions.

The recommendations didn't just focus on the management of the estate but also on the impact of Munro baggers and hill walkers. Montane habitats are highly vulnerable to damage caused by walkers, with trampling and path erosion impacting fragile plant species. This is why walkers are often encouraged to walk in single file along the tops. I had always thought tops were lifeless, scree-filled places, but these designations revealed inconspicuous and fragile high-altitude species.

The SSSI statement concluded with a series of objectives for management and outlined how the various habitats could be favourably maintained with an appropriate approach to muirburn, grazing and public access. The objectives focused on maintaining the montane habitat, the rarer species of plants and the breeding populations of merlin and dotterel. It very directly described how these objectives could be achieved: follow the Muirburn Code, manage appropriate levels of grazing on sensitive habitats, which includes controlling numbers of deer, make other grazing areas available for livestock; create fencing around sensitive habitats and maintain existing track and marking waypoints to direct visitors away from sensitive plants and breeding grounds. The final management objective suggested was to promote the understanding and enjoyment of the features that make the Drumochter Hills an SSSI through managed access.

I was surprised that the Drumochter Hills were home to some of the UK's rarest alpine plants and birds. Not only that, the combination of habitats and species was unique, and the hills therefore had international significance. I had naively assumed that any area with infrastructure such as trunk roads, hydro schemes or pylons must be low in biodiversity. These reports about Drumochter showed me otherwise. I found it even more confusing then, that the Beauly–Denny powerline had been given the go-ahead. I assumed it wasn't unusual for a traditional sporting estate to hold designations, but I had to ask what protection they really gave when given to private land.

5

The Stalk, Part Two

Target Practice

I don't need to pull the trigger.

Allan drives us to a stable block. He turns off the engine, opens the door, and I quickly follow him round to the back of the trailer. Ethan has stealthily materialised beside Allan, with the rifle unpacked. He passes it to Allan, who asks if I've ever used one.

'No,' I reply in a slight panic. I vaguely remember doing clay pigeon shooting near Aviemore as a child, but that's irrelevant. Allan begins to talk me through the rifle, describing the various parts of it, the scope, the velocity, but I can't take in much of what he's saying because I'm too busy panicking about what's coming next. He points at a target, a white rectangle maybe 100 metres away, and says something about lining up the crosshairs, taking the safety off, taking the shot and remembering to eject the shell casing. I stare blankly at the rifle. I have no idea whether I'll be able to hit that target, and what's worse than firing a rifle badly? Firing it badly at a living creature. I can't bear to think about the repercussions of maiming the hind – the suffering she'd go through and what we'd inevitably have to do to rectify my failure if, panicked and injured, she bolted with the herd. I feel my stomach drop at the thought of it. I can't, won't, let that happen.

I snap my attention back to Allan. He rests the rifle on the fence, where a seating platform has been built, like a hunting blind. I clamber over, and Allan brings the rifle to my right cheek. I rest the strange object against my shoulder. It feels solid, weighty. As I look through the scope, part of the rifle presses against my chin. It's cold and smooth. The rifle doesn't fit my body, and I have to adjust my positioning a few times before I feel in control of it. Allan asks me to look for the target ahead of us through the scope. I scan across the field with the little crosshairs for the white target with its black concentric circles. I find it and bring it into focus. I've to aim for the red dot in the centre.

'When you're ready, take the safety off,' Allan says. I come away from the scope to search for the safety catch. It's apparent that I missed Allan's initial demonstration, so he intervenes and does it for me. I look back through the scope and again line up the crosshairs with the little red dot. I suppress the residual panic from earlier and focus my mind, moving into a neutral state. This moment strangely chimes with the beats before you walk out on stage before a performance. I'm practised at acknowledging this feeling and pushing all the negative thoughts away, stepping over the threshold and submitting to whatever might happen. But today, rather than submit to a feeling of no control, I take charge of the moment. A deep steady breath in, then a calm exhalation, and as I come to the end of my breath, I squeeze the trigger and take the shot.

I'm caught off guard by the sudden rush of sensory input: the shock of the recoil pushing against my shoulder, the sudden shift of the scope that leaves me unable to see and the exquisite sound of the shot, like glass smashing at a high velocity. I hadn't anticipated what it might sound like so close to my ear. I listen to the tail end of its reverberation bouncing around us, ricocheting off the trees and buildings, skimming the surface of the loch and roaring up the hills, forewarning everything around us.

I regain my composure as Allan asks me to eject the shell casing. I didn't take that instruction in either, but Allan talks me through it this time. He then passes me the binoculars so I can check the target. I look and see that the red dot in the middle appears to have been replaced by a black dot, or rather, a hole. I couldn't have been more on target. Allan smiles at me. 'Pretty good.'

I feel a swell of pride. *I'm a good shot.* This is probably as close to a feeling of machismo as I'll ever get. I wonder if the stalker and ghillie are surprised: did a gender bias, subconscious or not, lower their expectations of me? My sense of pride subsides as I remember why I'm doing this. Nevertheless, I feel reassured and confident that I can dispatch a hind quickly, if I do it at all.

'Should I try again?' I ask Allan, assuming I'd get to practise a few times. 'You can, but that was good enough.' I'm persuaded by his confidence in me, and decide to push on with the day. Allan picks up the shell casing.

'This might interest you,' he says as he holds the casing up. 'We use copper bullets here.'

'Oh?' I respond, not realising the significance.

'Better for the environment than lead.' Bullet fragments can be found in the tissue surrounding a wound, and with parts of the carcass being left on the hill, it's very easy for other species, such as scavengers and raptors, to ingest lead, which can cause lead poisoning. This applies to any game that's not retrieved, such as rabbits or pheasants. Lead bullets are even more hazardous on wetlands as they corrode, poisoning waterways and waterfowl if ingested. In Scotland the use of lead shots over wetlands has been banned, and steel is often used instead. Copper too, being a non-toxic metal, doesn't pose the same threat to wildlife if ingested. I'm fascinated by Allan's revelation; the depth of thinking that goes into mitigating environmental damage is truly laudable. There are of course those that refute the efficacy of copper bullets as an alternative to lead, but, studies carried out in the field have found no difference in lethality between copper and lead bullets.

We pass Corrour Lodge, an imposing and impressive modernist building of granite, glass and steel, partially shrouded by trees. It's reminiscent of a villain's secret lair from a Bond film – definitely not what you would imagine a Highland shooting lodge to look like. The previous late Victorian lodge was destroyed by fire in 1942; this one was designed by Moshe Safdie, and was completed in 2003 on the same site.

We drive alongside Loch Ossian, which has an SSSI designation for black-throated divers, a species protected by the European Birds Directive. Allan asks why I've decided to go on a hind stalk. I explain about my time studying Sustainable Rural Development the previous year, and we discover that we share an alma mater. After studying ecology in Edinburgh, Allan went on to receive his deer-management qualifications from the University of the Highlands and Islands. We go on to talk a little bit about the perils of online learning. After a pause, Allan says, 'I thought you might have got the train here.'

'To Fort William?' I ask.

'No, to Corrour.'

Unbelievably, Corrour has a train station; it's on the Caledonian Sleeper Highlander route to Fort William. You can jump on the sleeper in London at 9.15 p.m. and be in Corrour by 9 a.m. the next morning. Indeed, not only is it one of the better connected Highland estates in Scotland, it's perhaps one of the more famous, though you might not realise it. Corrour Station featured in Danny Boyle's film *Trainspotting*, in the scene where Renton, Tommy and the gang decide to get out of Edinburgh for a walk. Tommy jumps off the station platform and marches towards the Munro in front of him as Renton bemoans being Scottish. His monologue about Scotland's status as a colonised nation being delivered on what would have been a traditional sporting estate at the time feels pertinent.

The sleeper train left 30 minutes ago, but there are still some people lingering around the station's restaurant and signal box accommodation. I look across the moor to the foot of the Munro with Renton's words weighing on my mind as Allan and Ethan unload the Argo from the trailer. The sun is just starting to catch the frost-tipped heather on this side of the hill, and it sparkles with a full spectrum of colours.

With the Argo ready, we pause at the railway barrier while Ethan phones for clearance to cross over the tracks, then we jump into the Argo and cross the railway line. The Argo is an eight-wheeled all-terrain vehicle that's used to access the various tracks around the estate. It's noisy, and fumes spew out the exhaust that extends from the bonnet. It has rollover protection bars and a canvas enclosure, but the sides are rolled up, allowing a clear view of the Munro. Allan and I share the front bench, and Ethan's riding in the open back with the rifle. Bumping along the uneven frozen tracks feels like being on a rollercoaster, but without restraints to hold me in. As Allan expertly and slowly navigates the steep troughs of the track, it sometimes feels as if at any moment we'll roll over. I have to hold onto the bar in front of me to steady myself. It's exhilarating but also hugely uncomfortable: this kind of vehicle is not made with petite women in mind. The bars I'm using to steady myself are in such awkward placement that I have to sit on the edge of the seat and contort my body to be able to hold one bar in front, and another down at my side. When the vehicle sharply tips to the left, I feel myself sliding along the leatherette bench towards the open side. I use my feet and brace myself against the sides of the foot well, locking my knees in position. Allan rights the Argo, and thankfully we're on a flat section for the time being.

As we lurch along, Allan points out peat hags, where the exposed peat is eroding. We talk a bit about the impact of the Argo on the hill. Argos and other all-terrain vehicles inevitably leave tracks that scar the hillsides. Many of these tracks were first created in the earlier part of the 20th century, specifically for stalking and other field sports, and usually to create a direct route from an estate's shooting lodge to the deer forest in order to avoid the long 'walk in' for guests. The tracks we're on haven't been created by clearing the ground with a bull-dozer, but they are inevitably wider at the boggier sections, and you can trace them all the way up the hill. These scars are visible across many of Scotland's landscapes, including in some high-profile areas of natural beauty. In 2018, MSP Andy Wightman led a campaign asking for these tracks to be subject to planning permission, particularly in our national parks and SSSIs. Today, they're more often created to enable better access and maintain infrastructural elements such as pylons, wind farms, hydros, logging roads and some popular hill-walking paths.

Driving up the hill feels strange: the summit above us is the hard-earned bounty of committed walkers, and here I am, sitting in an Argo, a collection of contorted limbs, cheating my way up the hill. The alternative would have been to walk from the train station, but that was never presented as an option. A century ago, we'd have had no choice but to venture out on foot, bringing ponies with us for carrying the quarry off the hill. Certain aspects of this historical way of stalking are still carried out on some Highland estates and in some of Scotland's national nature reserves. It would certainly have been the way things were done when my ancestors were gamekeepers 100 years ago. Today, I accept my role in this act of ecocide as we continue to lurch higher and higher into the fresh snow line.

6

Reclaiming

Hind Sight

In the course of my research, I came across an intriguing deer-management network called Hind Sight, created by Megan Rowland and Cathy Mayne as an educational environment away from the competitive and white-male-dominated spaces so common in deer management. Hind Sight aspired to be supportive, nurturing and enabling for women. In 2019, it brought together a network of women, ranging from professional stalkers to hobbyists and outdoor enthusiasts. Together, they would pool their knowledge of stalking and experiences on the hill, share skills and discuss outdoor equipment that wasn't merely a 'pink it and shrink it' version of its male counterpart.

It wasn't until a year after the hind stalk that I finally had the chance to chat with members of Hind Sight via Zoom. Megan was unavailable, so we arranged to talk another time, but Cathy popped up on my screen wearing a green zip-up fleece. Behind her was a framed photograph of a small herd of deer on a hilltop. She is a professional ecologist and deer stalker with a brilliant knowledge of plant species – her early career was in ecology and outdoor education. I was surprised to learn that it was only later in life that she had started stalking.

I asked her what the daily challenges were as a woman

working in land management, whether that be kit, attitudes or equipment.

'All of it!' she exclaimed. Their Hind Sight WhatsApp chat was full of complaints around clothing. Much of the kit for women was decorative rather than practical. It was designed with the assumption that any woman wearing it would be merely accompanying a shoot rather than fulfilling a profes- sional role. 'And rifles are made for men's bodies,' she said. 'The scope is a bit too far from my face.'

I thought back to the stalk and how I too found the rifle wasn't a good ergonomic fit. She admitted that the physical aspects of doing the job, like dragging the quarry off the hill and loading it into an Argo can be very difficult when you're physically smaller. Cathy could identify numerous ways in which the process of stalking and removing the quarry could be made easier with a bit of ingenuity. And she discussed how women couldn't compete on an even playing field when all the kit hinders rather than accommodates them. Suitable kit isn't available because there just isn't enough demand. Cathy estimated that there were fewer than a dozen women working as professional stalkers in Scotland. But the lack of good kit was also indicative of something much more concerning – that women were not considered part of the user group at all.

Some women found their way to Hind Sight after stalking or shooting with their spouses but felt they needed a space to nurture their interest outside of a male-dominated envir- onment. Cathy and Megan wanted Hind Sight to be a space that offers the opportunity to learn from more experienced women who have already found strategies to manage the bias and bigotry that can accompany deer management. Megan and Cathy were saddened to discover that many of the women in the Hind Sight network had experienced sexism and inappropriate behaviour on the hill. Cathy admitted that she would love for the group to be unnecessary.

I wanted to know more about hind stalking as opposed to stag stalking. Why, aside from the trophy aspect, were hinds deemed to be of less value than a stag? And what types of people would typically go hind stalking?

'They tend to be real hunters, people who hunt regularly. Hind stalking is more difficult,' Cathy told me. I was surprised.

During the hind-stalking season, she explained, hinds are naturally much more alert, in order to preserve their unborn calf or indeed any feeding calves they may have had late in the season. By contrast, in the stag season, which correlates with the annual rut, stags were usually more distracted by their drive to procreate or fight with each other, making the approach easier. It was the trophy aspect of stag stalking that made it more expensive, not the effort involved. Some of the women in Hind Sight were drawn to hind stalking because of the ecological benefits of deer-population management.

Incredibly, Cathy told me, hind stalking didn't exist 100 years ago.

The Coffin Road

Megan Rowland and I met some months later in Brora. I recognised her immediately. A young woman with elfish features, she carried a tall shepherding stick, similar to one my grandfather had. She and I had previously chatted over Zoom and Instagram and had exchanged some emails to organise the online chat with the Hind Sight group. Although we had never met in person, it felt like seeing a friend. I was eager to get her perspective on deer management in Scotland and the growing prevalence of 'green' landowners, who were arguably more ecologically minded.

We decided to talk and walk along the old coffin road from Loch Brora into West Clyne, a path that was used at one time to transport the deceased from surrounding rural areas to the cemetery at Clynekirkton. Coffins would often be carried by hand along the road, with rest breaks being taken at large flat stones known as coffin stones.

The coffin road nowadays is just a narrow track. Its verges were lush with vegetation, and branches of the young woodland skimmed the tops of our heads. It was an overcast, humid day and the sun strained to break through the clouds. The woodland was intercut with little waterways, over which hovered large damselflies and little blue butterflies. As we walked, Megan responded to every species we saw with a familiar sense of wonderment and appreciation. She commented on the quality of the woodland and the heather, which she saw would turn in a few weeks.

A few minutes into our walk, something wiggled wildly across our path. Both Megan and I stopped in our tracks and examined the creature. Megan put her hand down to gently stop its wild movements.

'A slow worm,' she concluded.

I was thrilled: this was my first encounter with the legless lizard that is often mistaken for a snake. It was desperate to find a sunny spot to sunbathe, so Megan and I quickly moved out of its way.

We emerged out of the woodland and onto the moor. The verges were thick with heather and some blaeberries. The track was dry and cracked, but it was obvious that it would make for a very muddy walk if it were to rain. As we ascended, the view of Loch Brora behind us became more picturesque. Ahead of us was seemingly never-ending moor and peat. Megan swung her stick in a wide arc to indicate where a new fence was going to be put in for deer management and eventually woodland. We went through a tall gate and into deer territory. As if to demonstrate this, Megan pointed out a couple of saplings on the verges that had been nibbled by the deer.

Megan has been a professional stalker for the past five years but had recently started an office-based job with a large environmental agency. As we chatted, she expressed concern at the way some agencies were looking solely at the numbers of deer and not their habitats. She told me that estates want an off-take of deer that is sustainable for their own stalks, but sometimes there was a lack of understanding, within both estates and agencies, as to how deer behave.

'If there's no space or shelter, for instance, the estates won't have stags. After the rut, they'll disappear, sometimes onto land with designations.'

This was one of the few times I'd heard someone talk about deer as if they had some agency of their own – that, despite their extraordinary adaptability, they had preferences. It made me reconsider the vacuum argument regarding the cull – the notion that deer would migrate into an area with lower deer numbers. In reality, if an estate failed to provide an adequate habit for the deer – for instance, if parts of the hill that provided the deer's main food source were fenced off and rewooded – they would simply leave, or worse, find themselves trapped in an area with insufficient food for their numbers. Megan explained that in this situation an estate might do a compensatory cull, and that sometimes only 10 per cent of land that is being rewooded could provide 90 per cent of the deer's winter feeding ground. Knowing how deer behaved within the habitats of an estate meant that land-management decisions could be made that supported both tree regeneration and deer stalking.

I asked Megan what else we rarely consider about deer. She talked about the estate that she currently lives on and where she used to work as a stalker. She had observed deer movements changing in the area over the last five years and speculated that this could be due to right of access granted to walkers in Scotland, or the rise in popularity of the NC500 route. More people were disturbing the deer, and there was a lack of knowledge about what impact those changes would have. We also didn't know much about the dynamics between red deer and other non-native deer species like sika. There was an assumption, Megan said, that different species would only hybridise when there was a lower number of available hinds of the same species, but this was just speculation rather than proven. She was a strong advocate for advancing our knowledge of deer to help us make choices in how we manage them. She even mentioned that deer could be used to mitigate against or avoid wildfires. She felt too that discussions around wildfires needed to be more prevalent within rewilding conversations. Shying away from controlled burns at a time when we're seeing devastating wildfires across the globe might not, in fact, be sensible.

We veered northeast, and Loch Brora disappeared behind us. We were completely surrounded by open moor, hills and sky. We approached a large, flat coffin stone. There was still no sign of Clynekirkton, and this stone must have provided some welcomed respite for those carrying the coffin. I imagined it as a pin in the landscape that transcended time.

I appreciated Megan's capacity to hold seemingly unbiased views on ecological restoration. Our conversations meandered from topic to topic, from conservation incentives and carbon credits to films like *Deer 139* and one of Megan's MSc research projects about beavers. I asked her why she thought deer were such an emotive subject in Scotland. She understood the reasons as being multifactorial; we had long projected value and cultural significance onto the animal. Deer brought value to estates and to the landowners who had the right to hunt them, but they had also been of value to those outside of the landowning elite, through poaching. Deer held spiritual meaning for our ancient people, and this is evident in Celtic folklore – deer were said to be both an omen of death in some circumstances as well as our guides through liminal space to the afterlife.

More recently, Megan felt conservation objectives had redefined how we valued, or rather didn't value, the animal, and deer had been misconstrued as a blight or vermin. Megan was frustrated that the conversation seemed always to be about what the deer represented rather than about them as a species in their own right.

I told her that I used to think estates could be understood as being either good or bad estates. To my surprise she laughed and agreed. 'There are some places that are doing a good job, that deliver good things, and have the research and data to back it up. Whereas some of them won't even engage in that process, won't do herbivore impact assessments, which is what Cathy does. And a lot of the estates that employ her don't do the assessments themselves; they don't know what's happening because their stalker is too busy mowing the lawn.'

This was really useful to hear: the difference between 'good' estates and 'bad' estates was more nuanced than I'd first assumed. It seemed obvious to me that stalkers and gamekeepers were well positioned to accommodate ecological science practices into their roles, but many were perhaps being asked instead to do garden maintenance around the guest accommodation.

The hills gradually parted in front of us, and the North Sea flooded the horizon. I realised that, as we'd been walking, Megan had never taken her eyes off the hills. She was always on the lookout for a herd, always on a stalk. As we descended into West Clyne, Megan and I began to talk more earnestly about the realities of the landowning elite leading restoration work. We thrashed our way through the thick bracken, and thrashed out our frustrations and concerns, eventually emerging triumphant at the walls of the Clynekirkton cemetery.

Women on the Streets

It was March 2021, the week of International Women's Day and Mother's Day, and the Reclaim the Streets movement was calling for vigils to be held across cities after the kidnap and murder of Sarah Everard by a police officer as she walked home. Women were coming out, once again, on social media to share their experiences of harassment and violence on the streets. I scrolled as friend after friend, colleague after colleague, stranger after stranger shared their experiences, their near-misses, the strategies they employed to feel safe – and the situations where those strategies had unfortunately failed them.

Tensions increased on 13 March as police officers forcefully removed women from a peaceful protest at the vigil held on Clapham Common in London. Protest boards were painted with slogans such as 'Stop killing us', 'Not all men but always men' and 'Boys will be ~~boys~~ held accountable'.

It was a week of contradictions, frustration and rage. We were told to stay off the streets, wear bright colours, share our locations, stay in after dark, challenge police officers, scream, carry an alarm. We were told we were powerful, but that we wouldn't be believed; that some of us weren't as worthy of respect, justice and freedom, but that we should be celebrated just the same; we were told to be kind to our mothers, but mothers were being murdered.

We were being stalked, and we were being told to adapt.

I read an article focused on the experiences of women walkers in the outdoors and their fear of male violence and harassment. Interestingly, most women interviewed said they felt safer outdoors in a remote or rural setting rather than in a city, although they would still use some safety strategies such as tracking apps for friends to access and would opt for campsites over wild camping.

The ways in which outdoor experiences differ according to gender is often apparent in nature books written by men. One book I read described a walk around the Knoydart peninsula in search of a particular bothy. On eventually finding the bothy, the male writer discovered two men already there drinking whisky. They obviously shared a dram, because that's what you'd do after a long day of walking. The writer opted to sleep outside the bothy in a tent, because there wasn't much space left inside. Up until that point, I'd thought about trying the walk for myself, but I knew my response to finding two men drinking whisky in a bothy would be very different to the writer's. I would be immediately cautious and would definitely not sleep in the bothy, or even within sight of it. This was sadly the conditioning that I'd received growing up as a woman. Encountering a man alone, especially somewhere with no phone signal, wasn't ideal. Encountering two men was worse. Encountering two men, a bottle of whisky and a communal sleeping space was a whole load of 'nope' with a side of 'absolutely not'. I am sure these kinds of scenarios have been a barrier for many women, me included, to feel comfortable adventuring solo.

That weekend, amidst the vigils, I was woken at 4 a.m. by an urban fox. I had a moment of panic, thinking at first that it might be a woman as the chilling, repeated screams echoed through the streets. I waited for something about the screams to change – the intensity or the intention. But they didn't. I lay awake and listened to the fox. Had anyone else looked out of the window to make sure it wasn't a woman in trouble? The foxes around our streets tend to feel safest under the cover of darkness; this is their time to reclaim the streets. Not my species though. I enviously imagined the vixen, padding around the streets at night, being loud, taking up space, drawing attention to herself without any repercussions.

Cailleach

I'd been thinking a lot about hinds, women, land and Celtic mythology. The belief that hinds were supernatural beings which could act as messengers, omens of death and guides through liminal space to the afterlife was most prevalent at a time when, in Scotland, a deer goddess cult was said to have existed. The deer priestesses were sometimes referred to as *cailleachan*.

I returned to the OS map of Drumochter and Cailleach Coire Chùirn. I had looked up the English translation of *cailleach*; it meant old woman, or hag. My curiosity was piqued: was the place name in Drumochter associated with an old woman or a deer priestess? One evening I typed various phrases into the search function of a portal for online academic journals. A decades-old article popped up, describing how the *cailleach* represented the life, wellbeing and fertility of the deer herd and tended to herds local to her region.

Cailleachan, although appearing as old women, were thought to be fey women, and deer were thought to be the cattle of the fey – or fairy – folk. The article recorded old stories of how *cailleachan* would transform into hinds, sometimes leading people to the otherworld. *Cailleachan* were usually benevolent unless provoked, but there was a common belief that should a hunter see a *cailleach* during a stalk they would go home with nothing.

Some *cailleachan* were regarded as a bad omen, apparently, particularly by those who benefitted from newly changed game laws. Landowners may have been granted the right by the king to hunt deer on their own land, but it was said that if they hunted without the permission of the *cailleach*, they would return empty-handed to the lodge. Ultimately the will of the *cailleachan* determined the outcome of the hunt.

The article referred to one specific *cailleach*, the Cailleach of Beinn a' Bhric. She was sometimes referred to as the deer priestess or the Lochaber Cailleach. I was especially curious after realising that the stories about her took place in Corrour.

I returned to the OS map, and sure enough, near Beinn a' Bhric, was an area named Fuaran Beinn a' Bhric. *Fuaran* means spring or fountain. I could see from the map that Beinn a' Bhric was adjacent to the hill that I had stalked on at Corrour. I wondered if Allan knew about these stories or of the *fuaran* that was referred to on the map.

The Cailleach of Beinn a' Bhric was said to live on the mountain; she would fish by hand at the north end of Loch Treig, and some had seen her take the form of a grey deer. One story associated with her told of how hunters would hear her sing as she milked her hinds. Once, a hunter who had had no luck hunting in the forests was sheltering in the evening when the *cailleach* came to him. She instructed him to watch her whilst she milked the herd. She told the hunter that the hind she struck while milking would be the hind he could take on his next hunt. It was believed that the next day the hunter went out looking for the herd and shot the very same hind she had struck.

Though most oral accounts of encounters with this *cailleach* were centuries old, one was as recent as 1917 – the gamekeeper of Corrour had shared a story of witnessing the *cailleach* cleaning out her well, and washing in it.

Intrigued by the connections between Celtic folklore and place names, I tried to find stories relating to the Cailleach Coire Chùirn in Drumochter, but there was nothing. It was frustrating. I knew from the census records that my family at Drumochter spoke Gaelic. Had they known the story of the Cailleach Coire Chùirn and shared it with their children? Did my great-great-grandfather attribute the success or failure of his stalks to the will of the *cailleach*? Did he have his own stories of seeing the deer priestess when out in the deer forest? I felt the loss of my Gaelic heritage, and I understood further the impact that cultural cleansing had had on the Highlands.

Although it was easy to feel romantic about the Celtic mythology surrounding the *cailleach*, I was wary. The myths illustrated the dualisms that othered women, aligning them with nature – and so, like nature, like deer, they could be conquered, captured or controlled.

7

Women on the Hill

Shortly after speaking to Megan and Cathy about the Hind Sight network, I watched a Scottish documentary film about the deer cull, in which Cathy was a contributor. I was already aware she had a wealth of knowledge, but the way in which she discussed deer management and biodiversity particularly impressed me. She delivered confronting truths that others were perhaps unwilling to say, but she was never scathing or dismissive of other perspectives. I was increasingly curious about this lone woman working on the hill, a kind of rare sage huntress. I reached out to her again, and we soon found ourselves together in the Highlands – in the middle of somewhere.

Earlier in the week, Cathy had sent me some OS coordinates for a Highland estate where she'd be carrying out some survey work and offered to let me tag along with her for the day. She told me to bring food, boots, waterproofs and a midge net, and it was a welcome relief to have someone tell me what kit I might need.

It was the height of summer, and the Highlands had been unusually dry and sunny following a late winter – there had been snowfall in May. The impact on many species and habitats, including agricultural land, was visible. There had been a noticeable drop in migratory bird numbers, with some birds not even laying a clutch that summer. I was soon to witness some of the other effects on the hillside with the help of Cathy's expert eye.

Cathy greeted me at the estate buildings with a big smile and an even bigger hello. She was unassuming, and her features had the glow of a woman who had worked outside for most of her life. We quickly headed off up to the hills where she would be working for the day. As it was a typical Highland estate, we drove on land normally only accessed for recreational purposes. We quickly left the main road and followed a single track up through forestry plantations, areas of natural tree regeneration, riverbeds, mountains and moorland. We headed out of the rocky glen and away from the tree line, up towards a huge concrete hydro pipeline that cut through the landscape. The track ran parallel to it; eventually we drove over the pipeline and zigzagged our way into the uplands of the estate. We stopped about 300 metres up the hill at a small sluice. At this point, the track was much less obvious and accessed primarily by Argos. In some sections, their tracks patterned the deer grasses, but they hadn't left much of a scar.

As soon as we jumped out of Cathy's vehicle, we were blasted by an unusually warm Highland wind. Although blustery, it was a welcome companion on the hill: it would take the heat out of the sun, essential in an area with no shade from trees, and more importantly, it would keep the midges and clegs, or horseflies, at bay. There was a bit of cloud cover, and the dappled light raced across the hills like searchlights, regularly bathing us in warm sunshine.

Cathy had received some criticism since the documentary had been released, and I asked her if she saw herself as a controversial figure. 'Not particularly. I just tell people what I see.' As soon as we got out of the car, Cathy switched into

educator mode. It was amazing to witness, and she was gener-
ous with her expertise.

We walked behind the car to what, to me, looked like an
old tree. The stump was white, gnarly, and appeared to have
clawed its way out of its peaty grave.

'Have you seen one of these before?' asked Cathy.

'Only on Rannoch Moor, I think.'

'This tree is thousands of years old.' Cathy rooted around
in the peat surrounding the trunk. She held up some ancient
bark. 'Yup, Caledonian pinewood. It's still visible because it's
been preserved in the peat. That's how we know the species
was present here thousands of years ago.'

We were witnessing deep time, natural history.

'This doesn't mean that trees should be planted here,
though,' warned Cathy. 'It just means that trees were here
before the peat. You can tell by the build-up around it.'

She opened the boot of the car and loaded up a rucksack
with various surveying paraphernalia: a digital camera, a mallet,
wooden stakes, what looked like climbing ropes, a GPS device
and a section of an OS map marked with dots and numbers.
I offered to carry something, but she preferred to know that
she had everything she needed on her. Cathy explained that
she was going to be surveying specific plots on the land to
assess the condition of the hill. She told me we'd be making
our way up and along the hillside before circling back to where
we started. I'd never participated in any survey work, so I was
keen to immerse myself in Cathy's world, to be another woman
on the hill.

Before heading off, I glanced around us. We were surrounded
by open hill on all sides. The landscape reminded me of the
hills at Drumochter except for one very important difference:
there were no grazing sheep. About a mile in each direction,

the hill gradually tapered up to form the peaks or plateaus of various Grahams. We strode out at some pace along the Argo track and carefully stepped from stone to stone over the burn which ran down towards the sluice. Cathy described what was around us. On one side of the track was mainly peatland, and on the other mostly bog, which was made up of even deeper layers of peat.

Cathy snapped off a bit of a plant and handed it to me. 'Crush this and smell it.'

I crushed the smooth waxy leaves and was hit by the smell; it was strong and pleasant.

'Bog myrtle,' Cathy told me. 'It repels midges.'

Then she stopped and pointed over to a small hummock. 'I can see from here that that's degraded.'

To me, it was indistinguishable from any other hummock. She marched us over to take a closer look. Cathy could see a lot of relatively new growth, which meant that at one time its vegetation had been removed.

She looked at the long stems of living heather then picked a stem of dead heather. It was woody and white: this meant something. I had no idea what, but it was obvious to Cathy. 'It's clearly been burned.'

It wasn't clear to me, but I felt disappointed that a destructive form of land management was used here. Cathy confirmed that muirburn was carried out on this estate, but in small patches. She could see it had been done really well in some areas – which I took to mean that this wasn't always the case. She explained too that muirburn can reduce the risk of wildfires. This felt particularly pertinent, as California wildfires were being reported and there were high summer temperatures across the UK. Only weeks before, a wildfire had occurred in Glenmore, in the Cairngorms National Park.

Cathy got down on her knees to take a closer look at the degraded hummock.

'It's also been heavily browsed.'

She could tell this by looking at the cross-leaved heath that had been left to grow; other more palatable species had been browsed back. Cathy was quiet for a moment as if diligently listening while the hummock told her its story of degradation.

Satisfied, Cathy strode off uphill, pursuing the GPS coordinates of her first plot. I followed and only caught up to her when she stopped to check her map. We had reached the first plot. Again, there was nothing to distinguish this area from the rest of the moor except its coordinates. Cathy heaved the rucksack off her shoulder and carefully pulled some of its contents out onto the heath. She hammered a marking stake into the peat so that the plot could be found again and reassessed. As the hammer clacked the stake down, I could almost feel the hundreds, maybe thousands, of years' worth of peat wobble beneath me.

Cathy found a rhythm with the hammer and spoke to me as she worked. 'The problem is. With leaving the stake too high. If you're a deer over there. It looks like a tree. Or something edible. Or if I'm a stag shedding velvet off my antlers. It's going to be great for getting rid of it. So you end up with. A circle of damage around the post.'

The stake sank through the peat easily enough until it met something harder. Cathy stopped and rummaged again in her rucksack, pulling out a saw. Within seconds the stake was at sward height, pleasing to Cathy and less interesting to deer.

'So landowners ask you to come and do this?' I was a little embarrassed at the naivety of my question.

'Their own estate staff could do this: the methodology is simple enough, but sometimes there might be a mistrust of science, or they're just too busy to do it. Having someone like me do it professionally gives value to the results. Especially if something unexpected comes up.'

Cathy went on to tell me about one high-profile job she had done: after three weeks of work, the estate disagreed with her findings. The assessment previous to Cathy's had shown high deer impact from winter browsing because of the condition of heather in the habitat, but what Cathy found were actually high historic impacts. The intensive burning and sheep grazing of previous years had led to a prevalence of purple moor grass and an absence of heather.

The methodology she had been using could tell her something about heather use but nothing meaningful about the wider habitat and the number of deer, nor the impacts they had on any other part of the habitat. Heather was not the only plant they ate, and deer could thrive in habitats where heather wasn't present. 'But we don't know what they're eating, because we haven't done the research,' she told me.

I'd never considered how historical impacts could skew the interpretation of contemporary impacts. But as Cathy talked, it started to make sense. I began to understand that deer might not be responsible for as much ecological degradation as we thought.

Unable to rely on heather, Cathy described the other indicators she used to try to assess how many deer there were in that habitat and how heavily impacted it was. She relied primarily on her tracking skills as a stalker, observing the amount of dung and looking at the condition of the deer in the spring. Through this alternative methodology, she was able to come up with a much more accurate assessment: low deer impacts, but high impacts on heather. 'It was a case of too little heather but not too many deer for everything else.' She was all too aware of how important it was to get this stuff right. Estates were making land-management decisions based on the information she gave them as an ecologist, so it had to be accurate. Fortunately, Cathy's experience and skills as both stalker and ecologist meant the estate eventually agreed with her findings.

Cathy delved back into her rucksack and brought out what looked like a tangle of rope. She unravelled it to reveal a kind of net that was actually a 2-metre square grid. She threw a knotted corner around the stake and pegged down the remaining corners, pulling them taut to create a plot. She carefully documented the GPS location using the cardinal points of the compass and noted down any landmarks. Then she took out her digital camera and snapped pictures of the plot from different angles to improve its chances of being found again. I awkwardly tried to get out of the way. Next, Cathy pulled out a sheet of paper to document her findings. Pencil in hand, she pointed to a small green plant with red hairs that protruded from its tips.

'Have you seen one of these before?'

I took a closer look and noticed little droplets that looked like dew sitting on the ends of its red hairs. I shook my head.

'Sundew. These are insectivorous: they eat midges.'

I gasped in delight at the news, and, amused by my visible enthusiasm, she told me that it wasn't the only species that did so. 'There's another one I can show you further up.'

My smile spread now from ear to ear.

Returning to her plot, Cathy pulled a peat probe out of her rucksack – which was reminding me now of Mary Poppins' carpet bag – and pushed it into the earth. The peat was not quite deep enough to be considered blanket bog, so she marked it down as a wet heath plot. She crouched over the delineated squares of the grid and began to talk me through the different species: heather, cross-leaved heath, deer grasses, cotton grass, bog asphodel, sphagnum and my new best friend, sundew. She kneeled in the heather, leaned over a quadrant and went quiet as she observed what each species was telling her about the condition of its habitat, from nutrients in the soil to which animals had been browsing. Cathy then measured the height of the heather and checked to see whether it was present in every square of her plot. It was. Satisfied, she wrote up her findings, and made some additional notes. 'It's very dry, very dry this year. There's some natural cracking and signs that the sphagnum's been disturbed. It's trampled. Deer are moving through here, but they're not eating the heather.'

Then she repacked her rucksack, checked the coordinates marked on her OS map and set off to find her next plot.

As we moved up the hill, the habitat subtly changed from peatland to bog. In some areas the peat was noticeably spongy and springy underfoot, though probably much less squelchy than normal this summer. But it often became hard and even crunchy where the sphagnum mosses were dry and the peat had cracked. I had come to learn that this meant the peat was in poor health, perhaps as a result of muirburn. Sometimes it was a sign that a drainage ditch was nearby. As we cut across the hill, we encountered several ditches with water streaming from the bog, leaving dry sphagnum mosses, degrading peat soil and ultimately causing carbon to be released. Peatland or blanket-bog restoration often involved filling in these ditches to rehydrate the peat and restore the natural flow of water and levels of soil saturation.

Cathy had advised the current landowners to consider restoring the peatland, but they hadn't yet done so. Along with Cathy's habitat assessments, she could provide recommendations, and even try to dissuade landowners from any unintentionally illegal practices she had seen evidence of on the hill. But it was up to the landowners and land managers as to whether or not they heeded her advice.

As we continued to trudge upwards, through heather and bog, being blasted by the warm wind, I felt an unanticipated sense of contentment. I was enjoying myself. I relaxed more into my conversation with Cathy, and we returned to discussing the diet of deer.

'See this thing,' Cathy said, pointing to a plant that looked like cross-leaved heath.

'It's supposed to be unpalatable to deer, but it's been browsed. We tell ourselves that deer don't like this, and that's come about from evidence, but the deer know what they eat and what they like. We don't really have thorough studies, except on Rùm, in which researchers follow deer around and see exactly what they eat. But we badly need them.'

'Do we know whether deer in Scotland follow something like a migratory route?' I asked, aware that deer in other countries with a much larger range are known to migrate.

'We have a view about how stationary or sedentary they are. Stags are mobile when they need to be, for the rut, and they'll travel tens of kilometres, but hinds are very sedentary and limited in their range. That's conventional wisdom, but it's not true for deer in woodland, and deer patterns of use do change over time. That could be because other land patterns change, or there could be a combination of factors that create a driver.'

Stalkers in general have a lot of knowledge and information about deer habits, and Cathy felt this needed to be captured somehow. But she found that stalkers were often 'salt of the earth' people who had spent a lot of time on their own on the hill, and they weren't necessarily interested in talking or writing about their experiences. I thought of the knowledge and experience that had inevitably died with my own gamekeeping ancestors and how I yearned for their stories.

Cathy stopped abruptly. She paused, quiet for a moment. She seemed uncertain about something. Then, with an edge of secrecy to her voice, she leaned down and introduced me to another species. 'This is one of the rarest plants in the Scottish hills.'

On the ground was a low, inconspicuous shrub, the dwarf birch. I was aware from my interactions with ecological restoration and rewilding organisations that this species was of huge interest, with many projects aiming to re-establish the dwarf birch in Scotland's montane habitat. So to see it here, self-willed, growing quite happily, without any human intervention, was a real privilege. Cathy told me that she had rarely come across it during her career. I watched as she gently touched its leaves.

Cathy explained that some landscapes were just not hospitable to trees anymore, and she began to talk about ecological restoration on a global scale. 'The Amazon now releases more carbon than it sequesters, so we need to do so much more than plant a few trees here. Much more useful would be to continue to nurture rural economic productivity which can benefit both environmental health and rural populations.'

Cathy wasn't saying we shouldn't plant trees, but she was emphasising that the scale of the issues we face globally far outweigh the mitigating effect of the tree planting we are doing in Scotland. She then cautioned against being uncritical of those whose business models rely heavily on exploiting the concept of 'wilderness' but are not globally sustainable. More than a few individuals of this kind came to mind, and I was beginning to see why Cathy could be regarded as a controversial figure. She called out the unsustainable and unethical practices of the global North, such as the export of our waste. My insides hardened as I imagined the mountains of plastic waste in places like Turkey and Malaysia. Planting trees in the uplands of the Highlands wouldn't resolve the issues with our approach to waste management: it could only assuage our guilt. As my diaphragm tightened, I could only respond to Cathy's points with sighs and yups of agreement.

'This restoration stuff allows us to be further distracted from dealing with the real issues,' she said.

I looked at the peat and heather under my feet and focused on softening the edges of my grief. Cathy let out a guttural roar of frustration. We both gave in and almost collapsed onto the hillside, our bodies caught and supported by the heather and mosses and ancient peat. I gently rolled the heads of the heather between my fingers and asked, 'Have you heard of the Coller Prize for Interspecies Conversations?'

The prize, hosted by the Coller Foundation, will award $1,000,000 to anyone that can 'crack the Rosetta stone of interspecies communication'. Cathy shook her head, looked to the sky and let out another low cry. She pointed to the face of a hill opposite us and recalled how the day before she had observed a group of hinds feeding their calves.

'You watch them, and you start to get an idea of what's going on, a very slight idea. But you're still looking at it from a human perspective. There's definitely communication, and we can get a tiny inkling of what that is. The problem is, the conversation the other way is, *Oh fuck there's a human! Run away!* Every single time.'

I smiled at how animated Cathy had become.

'Their conversation with us is always going to be, *I'm out of here, you're bad news.* They'll tolerate it if you're feeding them, but mostly, it's *I want to put as much distance between me and you as possible.*' Cathy let out a sad sigh. 'We are so the problem, and we so don't get it.'

The warm wind continued to rake over the hill, swaddling us in its raging white noise as if it were keening.

'How do you manage these feelings of grief, Cathy?'

'Not very well. Acknowledging them is part of the process, and resolving to do a little bit more about it. Having conversations is also valuable with people who share it. I am in the process of making significant life changes that are going to have meaningful reductions in my carbon footprint. I suppose the most useful thing I've ever done from a carbon point of view is to not have any children.'

I didn't ask Cathy whether this was through choice or circumstance. I didn't need to know.

'We're so divorced from our biological purpose in life that we're saying the most valuable thing that we, as women, can do, is to deny that. That's scary,' she added.

It is scary. And we were privileged to live somewhere where we had choices and rights, agency over our own bodies and reproductive systems. Many more women across the globe, of course, did not.

Cathy got back to work, and I felt the petrification of grief slowly retreat from my extremities back to my gut. She picked up her mallet and hammered another wooden stake into the peat.

After she had completed the plot survey, we continued to her next coordinates. I realised that I was looking at the ground differently, observing the variety of plants at my feet. With every step, I could name at least seven species.

'Can you smell that?' Cathy looked at me. I lifted my head and sniffed the air, flaring my nostrils. The wind quickly whipped away any distinct scent.

'Deer,' Cathy said with a smile. 'I can smell deer.'

I was dumbfounded. This was how attuned she was to

working on the hill. I continued to smell the air, hoping to catch a note of something unusual to me.

'What do deer smell like?'

'Tangy,' Cathy called back to me. 'The stags are tangy, more so leading up to the rut.'

We reached another plot, and, as Cathy worked, I scanned the landscape, looking for any movement, looking for any deer. I noticed the sway of overhanging vegetation of the peat hags, but other than grasses, nothing seemed to be moving. I looked in vain too for a shieling, or hut. There was a time when I would have assumed there was little evidence of people on this land. However, signs of our intervention and management were apparent to me now, even in the absence of a shieling. The drainage ditches, the historical sheep grazing, muirburn, cold burn, the hydro, even the lack of deer – all demonstrated human influence. I was reminded of Peter Cairns and his comments about ecological blindness. This landscape certainly wasn't desolate, but it wasn't wild either. The estate could be seen as 'good' *and* 'bad', well and poorly managed, healthy and unhealthy – the land could encompass all those concepts.

We set off again for the next set of coordinates. I asked Cathy if she'd ever been made to feel incapable as a stalker because of her gender. She didn't pause to consider her answer.

'Yes, partly because I'm not strong enough. But I've never had a problem being accurate and dispatching animals cleanly; that seems to be something women are really good at. I've not yet met a stalker who says women don't shoot better than men. It's to do with the fact that women are paying attention and are very conscious of what they're about to do. Men are a little trigger-happy, because the testosterone is charging round their system. We don't have that, and it's a real advantage.'

This assertion was of course based on Cathy's years of

professional stalking and taking clients out on the hill. I wondered to myself, though, whether the capability of the women Cathy encountered was down to a pressure not to fail, rather than a chemical advantage.

'I'm not a shy retiring type,' Cathy went on, 'and I've been taught to expect to be treated equally, so if I'm not I will probably say so or find a way to make it clear that I'm not happy.' Like many women stalkers and ghillies, Cathy explained, she'd experienced inappropriate advances from clients. She had found it easy to rebuff them, however – probably because she was holding a rifle at the time.

We reached the next plot. I asked Cathy about deer management in an area where ecological restoration and sporting estates bumped up against each other. I was thinking about Drumochter and Cairngorms Connect. Cathy absorbed the question for a moment, slowly unpacking her rucksack as she did so. I wasn't really sure what kind of answer I was expecting.

'The perception is that if you want to make an economically viable sporting model on a Scottish estate, you need a density of around twelve to fourteen deer per square kilometre, which is a little above what you would naturally have in most places, unless it's really good ground.'

Cathy hammered in the stake.

'From a conservation perspective, you might be looking at ten deer. Unless you want trees without fences. In which case, it would be between four and none.'

This remark about fences was most likely a reference to the work at Glenfeshie; the estate had taken the approach of not using fences and instead protecting its tree regeneration through strict culling. Cathy was not criticising this approach: she was merely stating the optimum deer density for it to feasibly work. I'd never really understood what the cull targets were, and knowing the optimal density for different land uses and approaches helped me understand the tensions that could exist between estates with different objectives. When I imagined the deer cull, I thought of it as a Scotland-wide, blanket approach to reduce total deer numbers. I hadn't appreciated the need to factor in the economic or environmental needs and objectives of any given estate, as well as its habitats or carrying capacity. This was why we needed more Cathys out on the hill, assessing the impact of deer grazing and the quality of the habitat and advocating for deer welfare.

'You have to ask the question: are we currently undervaluing our sport when we sell it? The only place in the world where you can shoot a stag on an open hill is here. There's no other open hill stalking in the world like this.'

I'd never considered that we might be underselling stalking. If anything, I'd always thought the pricing to be far too prohibitive for the likes of me and most of the Highland population.

Cathy finished her assessment of the plot, repacked her rucksack and threw it onto her shoulder with more ease than earlier. We continued to the next set of coordinates.

'There could be a model in which estates are compensated for having fewer deer. We also don't charge enough for stalking hinds. They're harder to hunt, and they're harder to select. You have to look at more subtle aspects of their appearance, which is pretty difficult to describe.'

There was a middle ground, Cathy thought: having lower deer densities and increasing the cost of stalking. I reflected on this. Arguably, stalking was financially inaccessible anyway. So what, I asked myself half jokingly, was another grand to those with an abundance of disposable income?

We stepped onto some healthy bouncy bog. This was Cathy's next plot. I pulled a mat out of my bag to sit on as

Cathy kneeled in the wet sphagnum and noticed some more dwarf birch.

'I worry that the conservationists have demonised deer, and that's very difficult to shift.' Her voice trailed off, and she pointed out across the land. A couple of hinds had appeared, and they were just close enough for me to make out with my naked eye. We watched as a herd of about 20 red deer slowly emerged. Cathy lay on her side in the moss, and I stayed as still as possible.

Towards the back of the herd, the mother hinds appeared with their fawns. They hadn't yet been alerted to our presence – a strong wind whipped across the stretch of land between us, carrying our scent away. We stayed low and very still and enjoyed the serendipitous moment. After an afternoon of discussing our heinous treatment of the planet, it was a relief to feel joy and wonderment fluttering inside my chest. I swallowed hard to keep it from escaping. The hinds slowly picked their way along the path of a dried watercourse, through the bog and up the hillside. One fawn had stayed especially close to its mother's side, and the hind was sure enough of her surroundings to stop and feed it in front of us. She stood and squatted a little to allow her fawn to squeeze under her and feed. Instantly its tail flicked back and forth in a frenzy of delight. Cathy watched through her binoculars, assessing the health of the herd. 'She's still got her winter coat, a slightly greyer colour. There's one of last year's calves.'

I watched through my much poorer quality binoculars and made hushed sounds of amazement every time another hind and calf appeared. They were completely at ease in their habitat.

'I've never seen anything like this,' I whispered to Cathy.

'This sight could be completely lost one day,' she replied.

101

The hinds and their calves slowly drifted away from us, up towards a bealach, or mountain pass, and out of sight.

Happy that the herd was now far enough away, Cathy began talking again. 'If conservationists pursue their agenda, we'll never be able to see deer like that in the wild again.'

Even with everything I had come to learn about deer management and ecological restoration, this thought left me feeling dispirited.

'They'd be harried so hard, you just wouldn't see them. They'd be gone.'

'Are the culling numbers lower than what conservationists want?'

'I think there's a happy medium.'

Cathy knew of estates that were active in ecological restoration and still fed deer, even though that seemingly went against ecological objectives. Winter feeding could reduce deaths that might occur from starvation, or because of an obstructive fence line. And tourists wanted to see deer.

Deer, through no will of their own, are burdened with satisfying our social, economical and environmental needs. Even mooted reintroductions of species such as lynx, sometimes framed as a solution to our 'deer problem', depend on the availability of deer. Is there any other species in Scotland that are so put upon?

The 'deer problem' in Scotland was first identified 150 years ago, but the rise in deer numbers has accelerated since then. At the start of the twentieth century, Scotland's deer population was said to be around 150,000. That number only accounts for red deer and not roe, sika or fallow, and dates from around the same time my family were at Drumochter. After the Second World War, at the time of the first Deer (Scotland) Act in 1959, the population dropped by a third to 100,000. The optimum population then was accepted to be 60,000. By the 1990s, the population had tripled to 300,000. If you added the other three species of deer, the likely population in Scotland soared to 512,000. In a 2016 report, it was estimated that the overall deer population could be 750,000, and it is possible that, presently, we have a population of a million deer. This increase is partly due to their extraordinary adaptability as a species. With our influence, deer moved to an open hill habitat, expanded their range and benefitted from our desire to artificially maintain high population densities. I dread to think what the situation will look like in a few more decades.

Scotland covers just under 78,000 square kilometres, including the islands. With an estimated deer population of a million, that means we already have a density of around twelve deer per square kilometre, which is what the cull aims to achieve in areas populated with deer. Some 40,000 square kilometres of Scotland's land, more than half of the country, is dedicated to deer stalking. If you placed the entire deer population solely in that area, there would be roughly 25 deer per square kilometre. To achieve a density of twelve deer per square kilometre within that deer stalking area, you would need to cull around 520,000 deer, more than half the estimated population.

It was clear from our conversation as we observed the hinds that Cathy had so much respect for this species. They were surviving in an inhospitable place. She had a theory that what she observed in our uplands was a result of people and cattle being taken off the hill. Before the mass increase in range and population of deer, upland habitats were carefully used in the summers for grazing. When people and cattle were eventually removed from the hill, they were replaced with Cheviot sheep, which grazed indiscriminately.

'The sheep reaped the benefits of the hill and absolutely

trashed it. And what we have is that legacy. The deer eventually came on to something impoverished. The habitat we see is so diminished, but it's not the fault of the deer we have on the ground now.'

I can accept that our damaged habitats are a legacy of historical overgrazing. I can also accept that deer aren't totally responsible, but a million deer is still a lot.

'Does that answer your question?' Cathy asked abruptly.

I struggled to remember what my question was, but no matter, we were on our way to the final plot. We headed downhill across natural watercourses and pools in the bog. We stepped down into peat hags and clambered back up onto the moor. We approached the last plot, and even I could tell it looked unhealthy, definitely burned, with lots of white heather stalks at ground level. It must have been a cool burn, however, because there were still heads on the heather stalks. No sphagnum, but we had come down in elevation from bog to peat. Cathy hammered the final wooden stake into the ground and talked about some of the larger membership conservation organisations and their approach to species and habitat management.

'Concepts like habitat corridors or habitat continuity are brilliant, but it depends what those look like and how you go about achieving them – and the price that needs to be paid for them. If it's to the detriment of a community's social, economic and cultural benefits, you want to think really carefully about that.'

It was always a relief to hear acknowledged the impact on humans and the notion that communities must be part of a process rather than simply having things done to them. Cathy mentioned this in light of the headlines that had come out earlier in the month regarding the actions of a new landowner at Kinrara Estate, on the edge of the Cairngorms National Park.

The landowner had been accused of putting rural communities at risk after instigating a carbon-sequestering 'lost forest'. This allegedly saw the estate's six gamekeepers being made redundant and evicted from their tied housing, which was put up for sale. Their actions had the potential to propagate widespread distrust of any landowner wielding green credentials. I had to admit that it unfortunately validated my concerns about the rewilding movement.

'There are only about 160 full-time keepers in Scotland,' Cathy told me. 'It's such a marginal number that maybe it's time to say goodbye. But they're largely families that have lived on the land for generations – you'll understand that.' Cathy looked at me as she said this. I guess I did.

Of course, Cathy didn't really think that we should be saying goodbye to gamekeepers. Many had adapted, usually at the bequest of the landowner, to become rangers, guides or even wildlife and conservation managers. So although duties evolved, their expertise was still of great value to an estate. And if these roles disappeared altogether, there could be a devastating impact on communities. Children would be taken out of already shrinking schools, and houses would be put into the holiday rental market or become second homes. Knowledge of the land and its ecological, social, cultural and historical significance could be lost as areas became dominated by tourism.

'The idea of dispossessing people of their cultural heritage is something that most people have quite a strong response to, and rightly so, because it's their identity.'

This last comment from Cathy prompted me to talk about Drumochter.

I had been looking at maps to rather literally find a way back to my cultural heritage, and it all felt so unsatisfying. I really valued my identity as a Highlander. But I'd spent the best part of the last year picking this apart, and as a result I felt lost. I just wished I could go for a walk with my family at Drumochter. Spend a day on the hill with them, like I was doing with Cathy.

Cathy listened thoughtfully and understood. She reminded me that my family might not understand the kind of agriculture we have today. They would have used forests or woods differently, for coppices or pasture woodland, for instance.

'We don't care for the land at all now: we use it. We have no respect for that natural connection.' The knowledge of that loss of connection was what made sitting here, together, on the peat so precious. 'We're not doing anything, we're just sitting on it, enjoying it, smelling it, seeing it, feeling it, and you eventually start to feel like your roots are going down.'

She was right. I felt connected, rooted, but I believed that feeling was mostly down to Cathy and the things she had shared with me that day.

She cast out her net for the last time and pulled the corners taut to form a grid for the last plot.

Afterwards, we had a bite to eat. We took a moment to appreciate the good weather and eventually heaved ourselves off the peat. Cathy patted all her pockets in search of her car keys. They weren't in their usual place. I started to worry slightly, and I looked back up the hill at the numerous locations they could have fallen out. At least we had accurate coordinates should we need to retrace our steps. After another pat down, Cathy confidently decided that they were back at the car. We plodded down the hill, back past the first plot, over the waterways, and soon reached the tree stump of the ancient pine and then the car.

The doors opened, and, as Cathy had predicted, the keys were inside.

She drove me a little way off the hill and dropped me off at the hydro pipeline. We said goodbye as I hopped in my own vehicle, and Cathy escorted me off the estate. It was a relief to finally be out of the wind, and I could tell I'd caught a bit of sun. I followed Cathy until she turned off to make her way back to the estate buildings. She gave me a big wave out of her window, and I suddenly felt sad that I might not see her again. Perhaps without realising it, Cathy had given me a gift: the ability to move gently through a landscape and not feel like an intruder.

8

Hollowing Out

Deer Carvings

My obsession with deer deepened following my time with Cathy and Megan. I looked for them everywhere, on the land, but also in the news. It so happened that, days later, the discovery of Scotland's first prehistoric animal carvings was announced. The carvings were found in Dunchraigaig Cairn, a burial cairn situated on the west coast of Scotland in Argyll. On the capstone of the cairn was an image of two red deer stags, with what were thought to be carvings of a deer herd. The carvings were thought to be Neolithic or Early Bronze Age, and what made them significant from an archaeological perspective was that, previously, stone markings of the same era discovered in Scotland were geometric in form rather than figurative.

When the cairn was first excavated in 1860, the carving on the capstone went unnoticed. I imagined the archaeologists squeezed into the cairn, lying face down, digging and scraping away at the floor, totally unaware of the hugely significant find above them.

It was thought that the carvings might indicate that a person of high status was buried in the cairn. Or perhaps the people buried there were the much mythologised Fiènne warriors, for whom deer hunting was a rite of passage. However, I like to think of the carving as being *for* the dead, not about the dead.

Perhaps, as in Celtic folklore, the deer were there to guide the dead to the otherworld.

Forget Landseer; the Dunchraigaig stags had arrived. And it was of no surprise that this oldest found animal carving in Scotland depicted deer. The carving reinforced, and perhaps even rationalised, the cultural and economic relationship we had with deer. It spoke to a different time, when the species represented survival, rites of passage, the supernatural, whereas today, it is emblematic of wealth, privilege and ecological degradation.

The theory around memes, or units of cultural transmission, as Richard Dawkins describes them, helps me to understand why the image of the stag is such a strong emblem for Scotland. For a meme to be successful, it has to be planted in someone's head, as an idea or as another replicable, transmittable unit, like a language or a song or story, which can spread from brain to brain. The meme of the deer as quintessentially Scottish or Highlandish has been replicated again and again throughout our society within rural economics, environmentalism, tourism, fashion, archaeology and even in the marketing of our foods. An abundance of company logos and brands include the image of a deer, or more specifically a stag, with its iconic trophy antlers. Perhaps the enduring strength of the meme reflects our ancient relationship with the species and the importance of deer in Celtic folklore. How would such a strong ancient connection with another species have impacted the way we've managed or understood our landscapes across the millennia?

Gaelic place names across Scotland allude to our historical relationship to deer alongside other species. Some suggest sites where deer would regularly congregate, such as Tòrr an Daimh in the Highlands. Others, like Meall na h-Eilrig near Drumnadrochit seem to be areas that were known to be useful as deer traps for hunting. I once made a list of the Gaelic place names around Drumochter, hoping someday to translate them, hoping that they too might reveal something about the ways in which my Gaelic-speaking family might have used or understood that land. The translations I pieced together as a non-Gaelic speaker were rudimentary. Much like the carved stags of Dunchraigaig, their meaning could only be assumed and not truly known. I was frustrated and bereft at being unable to access another facet of my culture, to feel so keenly the impact of a change in attitude towards Gaelic in just a few generations.

In Drumochter at the turn of the 20th century, it would no longer have been acceptable to speak Gaelic outside of the home. I never heard my grandfather speak it, though his mother and father would have done so to him, as had their parents. The idea, that transmissible meme, that Gaelic was no longer socially acceptable moved from brain to brain like a virus, until the language no longer existed, except in those who fought to maintain it.

Ecological Grief

Dr Sandra Engstrom is a lecturer in social work at the University of Stirling, and I contacted her after reading articles in which she discussed the intersections between social care, climate justice and ecological grief. I couldn't believe how fortuitous it was to find an academic in Scotland who was publishing work on these topics. After some enthused emailing back and forth, we agreed to meet in Stirling at the university campus.

In my research, I had been surprised to learn that the discourse around ecological and climate grief was being partially driven by academics in social sciences. I associated the concepts with environmentalism and not social care specifically. But there was a growing body of research that acknowledged the detrimental impact on our mental health of increased occurrences of environmental destruction and disaster events. Typically, ecological grief occurred when we experienced the loss of a place, an environment, a species or a habitat. It happened as a result of destruction witnessed on any scale, from the HS2 development to huge natural disasters that destroyed entire communities, such as wildfires. The initial distress caused by these ecological events was known in the field as solastalgia, which was made worse by feelings of powerlessness or lack of control.

Sandra was warm, with a friendly North American accent, and she cut a laid-back figure in denim and aviator-style sunglasses. We decided to walk around Airthrey Loch, which was created in the late eighteenth century as part of Airthrey Castle's landscaped grounds. In all my time at the campus I had never walked around the loch proper, and in early summer everything was coming into full bloom. The gravel pathways were lined with long grasses and cow parsley, the rhododendrons were flowering pinks, purples and corals, and the lochs were covered in water lilies.

Sandra talked about her interest in the emotional experiences related to climate change, how they encompassed both the newer concept of ecological grief and the trauma of experiencing large-scale disasters. She discussed how humans need green spaces for mental health, yet there was paralysis when these green spaces changed or disappeared. She wanted to understand how we could sit with that duality and manage the impact of climate change on our mental health. I described to Sandra how I had only recently come across the terms climate grief and ecological grief. Although they seemed inherently linked, there must have been a nuanced difference.

'I think the term ecological grief places us within that ecological system,' Sandra said. 'It's a recognition that ecological destruction also means our own destruction. Like biophilia – the recognition that we are as much part of the natural world as anything else; the trees, the grass, the annoying midges, we can't separate ourselves from it. So much of our day-to-day life is removed from that connection, and it can seem a foreign concept to a lot of people.'

A swan had appeared on the path in front of us, and it did not look happy. By the path was a clutch of cygnets and another parent swan. We backed away and instead took the long way around the loch.

I was fortunate to already feel a connection to the natural world, even if I didn't understand it as biophilia, which, Sandra explained, is the emotional connection that we experience with other living organisms and the natural environment. It is not just an emotional connection but also a biological one: it helps us to survive. We're naturally drawn to environments that can facilitate our survival, with resources such as fresh water, food and shelter. Some think this is why we generally perceive greener neighbourhoods as being safer, because green spaces would typically have these essential resources. That said, parks and green spaces aren't necessarily safe spaces for much of our society, particularly after dark.

Research suggests that our connection with nature and the opportunity to indulge can give us the emotional resilience to tackle everyday life. I thought about Ben Wyvis, and how my morning commune with the mountain was intrinsic to my emotional wellbeing.

'The concept of us being a part of the natural world might feel a stretch, as might the concept of biophilia,' Sandra continued. 'Some people might be so removed from the concept that they'll need other steps, conversations and actions to get to that understanding, so for some it's more of an end point than a starting point. Though we may not consciously experience biophilia every day, it's apparent in our values and our hobbies, in the way we spend time outside. We can know when it feels good, when it feels right, when it's supporting us.'

Knowing the term biophilia gave me a much better understanding of how my relationship to the environment could be a huge part of my identity. It made sense that the further away we find ourselves from natural environments, the further we are from ourselves.

According to Sandra, ecological grief can come about when a person's biophilic connection to nature is undervalued, unrecognised, compromised or severed. She described the trauma she'd experienced when several friends died as a result of accidents in the mountains. Subsequently, she had had trouble reconnecting to the natural world and found herself unable to travel to the mountains for a period of time.

'It took a good ten years to recover. It was a slow reintroduction. I had to question who I was now. Who were the mountains now? I felt we, me and the mountains, had to test this new relationship: they were usually my safe space, but sometimes they were not.'

Sandra was interested in how the inherent risk in outdoor pursuits affected our understanding of our interactions with the natural world. She remarked with curiosity on the culture of Munro bagging in Scotland, and how the same thing wouldn't be possible in Canada. The mountains are too high, too hard, but more than that, 'We don't grow up thinking we have to get to the top of everything, and conquer the hills. It's interesting, but I don't like to engage with it.'

I admitted to Sandra that I too didn't engage with the

competitive side of walking. It really put me off, that awkward feeling of hearing someone at my heels when I was trying to avoid an asthma attack.

'In the Rocky Mountains, it just isn't an option. You learn to value just having a good day out, just being engulfed by the mountains, being outside.'

Fortunately, Sandra found her way back to nature, and also gained a new level of respect for the natural world. Her story helped me to understand that ecological grief wasn't always caused by mass ecological destruction or a natural disaster. It could also be caused by a single devastating event. It wasn't surprising then that social work was perhaps best placed to support this grief and mend our relationships with the environment.

Sandra and I passed the football pitches at Castle Law, where Dumyat, a low summit of the Ochil Hills, came into view. The lower sections of the hills were dappled with yellow whin bushes, heavy with the scent of coconut at that time of year. We wandered down into a small mature broadleaf wood and gradually up again towards Airthrey Castle.

Our conversation turned toward some of Scotland's most iconic scenic locations, our desire to experience them and the attachment we often feel towards them. 'To me,' said Sandra, 'place attachment is the emotional and, in some cases, spiritual, connection we have with either a built or natural environment, a place to which significant, usually positive, memories connect us, and an understanding that part of who we are, part of our identity, is linked to that place.'

In Canada, Sandra told me, a truth and reconciliation process includes the repatriation of land to indigenous peoples. 'They were removed from their land, but their connection to their ancestors, their sense of self and their history is rooted in that land.'

This reconciliation process has seen land returned to indigenous communities in some cases, and traditional indigenous territories are often recognised with a territorial or land acknowledgement before a meeting, conference or ceremony. Sandra laughed. 'If that were to happen in Scotland, it would blow my mind.'

I considered what a land acknowledgment might look like in Scotland but struggled to imagine anything before the feudal system of land tenure.

Sandra noted that place attachment is developed through interactions in the past, whether negative or positive. This helped me understand why the Clearances have felt so intrinsic to Highland culture for me. The mass de-peopling left physical and emotional legacies and directly impacted the Scottish psyche. Communities lost not only their homes, land, and work but also their identity. This could be why Scotland now has a growing uptake of community land ownership. Granting communities autonomy over their land holds potential for positive future interactions and could ultimately restore a sense of self and cultural identity.

Airthrey Loch came back into view, and another family of swans glided across the water towards a floating barrier, in place to try to control the invasive, non-native water fern. The plant can create a dense mat of vegetation on the water and prevent light from reaching other aquatic species. We reached the lochside path again. I noticed, on the other side of the water, the mother oak from which I had previously collected acorns. Only one out of the three had germinated at home, and I was on the lookout for a suitable habitat in which to eventually plant it.

Sandra introduced me to an ancient decision-making concept used by some indigenous people: the Seventh

Generation Principle. 'Not many of us think about what our great-great-great-great-grandchildren will be needing. But we need to rethink time in that way, taking ourselves out of the equation.'

I thought about people like Cathy saying that we wouldn't see or experience the benefit of the trees we plant in our lifetime.

'We need to consider our slow-time response,' Sandra continued. 'What do we do between moments of fast response? When we need to build resilience, how do we get people to think longer term? A few of us thought the pandemic might be the impetus for change, but so many people want to simply go back to what was. If that didn't cause people to rethink how we're doing things, what is it going to take to really make people realise that we're more connected and integrated with the natural world than we generally assume?'

As we headed back towards the main part of campus, I knew our conversation would shortly come to an end, so I steered the conversation back round to ecological grief. I ended up asking what felt like a desperately personal question, a cry for help, almost.

'How do you think ecological grief might be managed or overcome in someone you might encounter in a care setting? Obviously I'm asking for a friend.'

Sandra laughed, taking the edge off my discomfort. 'What I've learned from other grief is that it never goes away. You can't "action" your way out of it. It can be overwhelming, even paralysing, but you have to live with it and use it to help shape the decisions you're going to make in life.'

I found this a little confronting. I'd never considered that I would have to live with the grief and grow to accommodate it. I suppose I thought that it might eventually turn into anger or hope, or some other more useful emotion.

'Engaging in the conversations is a solid first step. You're gaining awareness, understanding how it is, how it feels, the label of it. Now you need to figure out how to live your life.'

She listed some of the ways in which to manage it, the choices that could ease the feeling of grief – buying secondhand clothes, being aware of where food comes from, litter-picking, foraging for mushrooms. How, through our own habits, we can gently influence others. Sandra mentioned some of the things an eco-therapist might advise as ways to reconnect with the natural world: sitting still outdoors for long periods of time, walking barefoot on sand or grass, caring for a houseplant. When she personally needed to feel reconnected or grounded, she would find a spot in nature and sit still.

We parted ways, and as I made my way back through the campus, Sandra's words were racing through my mind. The grief I felt didn't feel the same as grieving a person: it wasn't as if something was missing and my life was suddenly different because of that. Rather, the grief felt accumulative. I started to wonder when this accumulation had begun, when my relationship to nature might have changed. Had there been a specific event? It occurred to me that there had been.

When I first left the Highlands, I moved to a big city in the Central Belt for university. For years I struggled with what, at the time, I understood as being homesick. Indicators of the shifting seasons were fewer in the city. In March, I no longer found tadpoles in puddles. In May there was no cuckoo to listen for. In early winter, I didn't see the snow creep down Ben Wyvis and across the Black Isle.

I remembered having a session with a student services counsellor at the time, where I talked about this and how I hoped things might feel better because the otherwise terrible accommodation I had recently moved into had a mature tree in the

117

back garden. The counsellor had looked at me with what felt like derision. I was desperate for someone to understand what I was experiencing, but instead I left feeling foolish. Instead of resolving these feelings, I buried them and got on with city life. It wasn't until nearly ten years later, when I read *Feral*, that I started to rekindle my relationship with the natural world.

Mourning

In the global North, ecological destruction didn't always feel as dramatic or tangible as events such as the bleaching of the Great Barrier Reef, the continued destruction of the Amazon rainforest or the disappearing islands of the South Pacific. Not feeling the impact of the climate crisis so acutely was one of the many privileges we experienced in Scotland, although we had experienced a longer winter and a drier summer, the impact of which had been visible on the hills with Cathy and Megan. Researchers warned that many of our low-lying island and coastal communities would soon be impacted by rising sea levels, and flooding would continue to increase in scale and occurrence.

This was beautifully and starkly illustrated through a light installation in Lochmaddy, Uist entitled *Lines (57° 59' N, 7° 16' W)* by Finnish artists Pekka Niittyvirta and Timo Aho. The buildings in the community were wrapped with a single tube of light that indicated the anticipated level of high tides in the future. The climate crisis was impacting Scotland already; it was just that our species, so far, had the ability to adapt. Those species that couldn't were being hardest hit. For the salmon and other freshwater species in our rivers, warmer air and less riparian tree coverage meant warmer river temperatures. Parasites, bacteria and algae thrived in higher temperatures, and the altered biome of the rivers impacted the health of freshwater species.

During the 2019 Edinburgh Festival Fringe, I saw a show by science journalist and writer Alanna Mitchell called *Sea Sick*. During the performance, she described the chemical changes in our oceans. She took her audience on a journey to the bottom of the ocean and described the dead zones she had witnessed, where no life could exist because of deoxygenation. After what was a harrowing hour, I felt both devastated and reassured. Listening to someone else as they documented their journey through their ecological grief consoled me and made me feel less alone. I decided to stay for the post-show discussion. Mitchell came back on stage to chat with the remaining audience. I tried to pluck up the courage to ask a question. As I rehearsed it over and over in my head, I could feel my heart rate go up, and I broke out into a cold sweat. Eventually, I raised my hand, she pointed in my direction, and in a shaky voice I asked how she managed her feelings of ecological grief.

'What you're feeling is very difficult, but I don't feel grief anymore,' responded Mitchell. 'I feel hope, and I act.'

That seemed so far away from my own experience. She hadn't just *found* hope, she had chosen it as part of her call to action for the planet. Mitchell's words were powerful, but I just wasn't there. I hadn't yet chosen hope.

*

Prior to my meeting with Sandra, the grief I had felt for habitat loss and ecological degradation felt like it wasn't valid. And yet, humans are clearly capable of mourning the loss of people, places and species without being in proximity to them. We can mourn across time and space; there is seemingly no limitation to our capacity for grief. If we are collectively capable of feeling grief for the loss of life on the other side of the world as a result of events such as war, natural disasters or police brutality, then we must be capable of collective grief for the loss of non-human entities at a distance too. That said, humans are also capable of deeming some bodies less worthy of grief than others, whether because of their race, religion, ethnicity, gender identity, sexual orientation, class, immigration status or health. According to intersectional ecofeminist thought, the systems that determine this disparity are the same that result in non-humans being seen by some as less worthy of our grief.

The value, or lack of it, placed on non-humans is illuminated by considering the example of trees as a resource. Although trees hold huge value within an ecosystem, stabilising soil, absorbing water, sequestering carbon, distributing nutrients and providing shelter, shade and food for other species, they are not deemed economically valuable until they are cut down. And in terms of loss, some trees, like some humans, are deemed less worthy of grief than others – those purposefully grown to be a commodifiable source of fuel or timber, for instance. The expectation is that we won't miss or mourn these trees when they are removed.

I struggled to imagine an appropriate way to mourn the loss of habitat, species and places. Others created memorials, held vigils, protested, fundraised or replanted. I thought perhaps my mourning could be addressed through culture and art. Alanna Mitchell's work had resonated so deeply with me. Another artwork that came to mind was Beatrice Searle's *Foregathered wi' the Beast*. Searle, a stonemason and artist, had created a guerrilla tribute to the last wolf shot in Scotland – a large memorial stone installed north of Brora at the side of the A9, expertly carved with an inscription:

IN MEMORY OF THE
WOLVES

PART OF THESE LANDS
LOST TO GENERATIONS

WE AWAIT YOUR RETURN

Searle's memorial stone was laid opposite the older Wolf Stone, which marks the supposed site where the last wolf of Scotland was killed in 1700 – its inscription reads more like a celebration of the extinction event. Searle's stone acts as a reminder of what we had lost and what we could still lose; it offers solace and a much needed alternative perspective. The site has become a place to mourn the ecological loss of the wolf in the Highlands.

The Tree

After meeting Sandra, I took time to reflect on my own biophilia and place attachment to where I grew up. One area of Inverness I lived in had, at the time, only ten residential properties and a population of around 40. However, within fifteen years, the population had exploded to nearly 3,000. The area was transformed from fields of crops lined with copses to huge housing developments with their own roads, amenities and even a school. When I was even younger and living in Inverness itself, my daily walk to and from primary school passed through fields of carrots, neeps and tatties; those too were eventually handed over to developers. It was no lie that Inverness was one of the fastest growing cities in Europe. Perhaps seeing these fields turned to housing was the root of my anticipatory grief later in life for the outdoor spaces I enjoyed so much – grief for potential future loss, for something that had not happened yet.

Near my home on the outskirts of Inverness was a large tree. It was the sort of tree we would all be drawn to, I hope, as children. A dependable, solid, climbing tree. I loved to climb its branches, hang upside down like a sloth from its boughs or perch higher up and look out over the fields, my arms dangling over the branch above me. Sometimes I would just sit quietly and watch the sunset gradually behind Ben Wyvis. So important was this tree to me, that one day I even made a figurative carving of my teenage nickname, *Fairy*, into the tree's dense truck. I had recently wondered if it too might one day succumb to the developer's bulldozers, and after my conversation with Sandra, I decided to take positive action to tackle my anxiety about its future loss.

I discovered that the Woodland Trust held an Ancient Tree Inventory, which enables members of the public to record the locations of ancient trees across the UK as a means to care for and protect them. I headed back home to visit the tree and to gather some data for the inventory. It was a damp drizzly summer evening when I ventured out with my dad, up the path to the tree. I told him what I was up to, and he knew exactly which tree I was referring to. One of his friends, he said, had volunteered with the trust to verify the trees.

We almost couldn't find it for its dense foliage. It was even bigger, and its boughs had started to lower themselves to the earth to support its weight, just like the old oaks in the grounds of Knepp Estate that Isabella Tree described in her book *Wilding*. Underneath its boughs, I noticed dens had been constructed using the fallen sticks and branches. It was clear the tree was just as important to the young people that lived here as it was to me when I was young.

I found where I remembered making the carving, but it had been swallowed up by the expanding trunk. Its girth was so large that I couldn't wrap my arms around it. I unrolled the measuring tape and marched around the trunk, noting its circumference – 3.5 metres. Next I had to confirm the species. I walked away from the trunk toward its lowered boughs and examined the leaves, expecting to see the familiar wavy edge of oak. But they were oval and corrugated. A beech. In disbelief, I checked the ground and found a carpet of thousands of brown bristly cupules. Definitely a common beech. For all those years, I'd thought it was an oak – I suppose because of its size, and because I didn't know that beech trees could lower their boughs. But I've since found out that a beech can grow to be 30 metres tall with a girth of up to 6 metres and is comfortable in the same habitat as an oak.

Back at home, I added the data to the online inventory. A tree-age calculator suggested that, based on its girth, the beech could be 205 years old. Given the history of the area, this was a very fortunate tree. A map from the 1880s showed that a few hundred metres further down the burn was a sawmill. I wondered if the mother tree had succumbed to it, leaving her sapling behind. Registering the tree felt like a positive action, a little spark of joy.

The next day, the morning news told of an underwater gas pipeline that had ruptured, causing a raging inferno in the Gulf of Mexico. The story broke with apocalyptic aerial images of the ocean bubbling with flames, like some kind of portal to hell. In an act of self-preservation, I didn't read any more about it. It was hard to feel hope when the world was literally on fire. I remembered Sandra's advice about managing the distress that ecological grief can bring, and I walked myself back up the path to be with the beech tree.

9

Ryvoan

It was my last day in the Highlands for a few weeks, and I'd arranged to walk on the Ryvoan trail in Glenmore with Jeremy Roberts from Cairngorms Connect. When I looked the trail up, I realised I had walked it 20 years earlier on a school camping trip to Badaguish. I had memories of traipsing along the track in relentless horizontal rain, eventually reaching the bothy to shelter for lunch. After a short break we had continued up the adjacent hill in the rain and mist. Once at the cairn, I remembered a few of us had decided that the quickest way down was to roll like logs down the hillside into the mist, much to the horror of our chaperones. We eventually made it back to the camp at Badaguish for a soggy BBQ, where I ate venison for the first time.

I smiled at the memory of the camping trip as I headed through Rothiemurchus and eventually passed the sign for Badaguish. The unbelievably good weather combined with international travel restrictions had drawn a huge number of tourists to the Cairngorms National Park. I'd never before seen so many cars parked bumper to bumper on the verges along the full length of Loch Morlich.

I arrived early to meet Jeremy at the Glenmore car park. The sun was already giving off a fierce heat, and the wind had dropped completely, creating the perfect conditions for clegs.

As I waited, several families arrived. They tumbled out of their vehicles with kids and dogs and prepared to head up into the Cairngorms with walking poles or bikes.

A car with Cairngorms Connect decals on each side pulled into the car park, and I walked over to meet Jeremy. He immediately came across as affable and reminded me a little of Peter Cairns, whom I knew was a friend of his. My legs were covered and already itching with cleg bites from earlier in the week, whereas he was wearing shorts – brave man. He pulled some large A1-sized boards from the boot of his car and laid them on the bonnet. Printed on them were maps of the 60,000 hectares of the Cairngorms Connect partnership, highlighting the individual landowner partners within it – Wildland, NatureScot, Forestry and Land Scotland and the RSPB. The partnership was focused on the west side of the Cairngorms, not the east, which was mainly blanket bog and peatland. It was clear from the map that the biggest partner in terms of size of landholding was Povlsen's Wildland with Glenfeshie Estate; the smallest was NatureScot, which, together with Foresty and Land Scotland, jointly managed the Invereshie and Inshriach nature reserve. I wondered to myself which partner held the greatest influence and power.

Jeremy showed me the route we'd be walking. I'd been fortunate enough to enjoy a lifelong relationship with the Cairngorms landscape, and I was curious to find out more about what the partnership was doing in the Cairngorms and how my relationship to this landscape might evolve and change.

'Ecological restoration' best described the work of Cairngorms Connect, Jeremy explained. 'As a partnership, we're very clear: we're not here to criticise other land managers. All we're doing here is saying, we've got something that's already pretty amazing, we happen to be in a really good position to enhance it, and, in doing so, we think it's going to give benefits to wildlife and to people.'

He appreciated and understood that opposition to rewilding and ecological restoration was driven by economical, cultural and historical factors. Not all land managers liked the Cairngorms Connect model, and he accepted that other land managers local to the partnership would continue to practise driven grouse shooting, commercial timber planting or commercial agriculture.

I knew there was some opposition to the high cull numbers at Glen Feshie, and I had seen Jeremy discuss this before in a community context. There were debates about how the cull would impact adjacent estates. As the partnership didn't have fences, was the cull creating a vacuum that would draw herds away from the surrounding sporting estates? I remembered what Megan had told me about stags: if estates didn't meet their needs in terms of space, food and shelter, they would just leave and go elsewhere. This concern showed an awareness of how a change in one area impacts work on a wider scale. But it didn't seem very self-reflective to me. Were land managers asking themselves how their driven grouse shooting impacted adjacent estates? Or how the run-off from their fields affected the River Spey? Could these land managers or estate workers see the benefits of being adjacent to a habitat that was being restored?

Jeremy had considered this himself. 'Sometimes they don't perceive the benefits, or they are so fundamental in their views that they have no intention of seeing any benefits.'

One significant draw to the area that the partnership covers were the forests, particularly the remnants of the ancient Caledonian pinewoods. Jeremy told me that in order to protect these remnants and, in addition, the natural regeneration, reforestation and afforestation, and to avoid putting up fences, they needed to control deer numbers. Other growing trends that were bringing people to the area were wild swimming and paddle-boarding in the lochs and rivers around the National Park. The natural filtration processes of the forests and peatlands around the lochs and rivers ensured a high quality of water, and the salmon fishing in the area was dependent on the riparian forests that kept the water at a cool temperature. Even farmers in the lower catchment of the River Spey benefitted from the slower flow of the water as it moved through the National Park and reduced the risk of flooding.

'Those are all benefits, and I suspect a lot of people are unaware of them. I think we've got a job to build that awareness.'

Jeremy pointed out the undergrowth, or understorey, of the forest as we followed a fairly wide gravel track up through a plantation of Scots pine. Unlike other plantations I'd walked through, the understorey here had an abundance of blaeberry and heather. Normally, as the pines grow and the crowns fill out, the canopy becomes too dense for sunlight to penetrate the understorey. However, the partnership thinned out the plantations, allowing more light to reach the understorey, thereby allowing for more biodiversity. Jeremy, adept at demonstrating his point, directed my attention to the Norway spruce plantation on the other side of the track. The understorey there was dark by comparison, with the odd bit of grass growing but no heather or blaeberry. When we first started out on this track, I'd already written off this area of plantation as the bit to walk through before reaching the more impressive areas. But the partnership saw the potential for enhancement everywhere.

We reached a more thinned-out section of the forest, and the wide crowns of 'granny pines' sat on the hillside. These Scots pines, remnants of the ancient Caledonian pinewoods, looked resplendent bathed in the morning sunlight, each with an abundance of space around their aged branches. To protect these rare remnants, the partnership removed non-native plants from them, such as any regenerated Norway spruce. This might have seemed counterintuitive, but mature Norway spruce was prolific in comparison to the ancient Scots pines.

'We have over 5,000 recorded species in the project area,' Jeremy said. 'Of those, 20 per cent are nationally rare or scarce. Scots pine is important for species like capercaillie, twinflower and the narrow-headed ant.'

One of the unique aspects about the Cairngorms Connect area, Jeremy told me, is its altitudinal range – from 200 metres above sea level on the flood plain of the River Spey to 1309 metres on the summit of Ben Macdui, Scotland's second highest Munro. Jeremy pointed to a hill on our left; it had a ridge with a defined peak. 'Meall a' Bhuachaille, Hill of the Shepherd,' he told me. The Gaelic pronunciation rolled off his non-native tongue with aplomb. I wondered for a moment whether this was the hill we had rolled down as teenagers. If so, I could now appreciate the horror our chaperones had experienced.

Jeremy handed me his binoculars and told me to look through a gap in the trees toward the top of the hill. I could see lots of young trees marching, as he put it, up along the ridge towards the peak. I didn't understand the significance. He then directed me to look to our right, at the ridge of another hill. It too had little trees marching up the hill. The significance was still lost on me. I made positive sounding noises. Perhaps it was natural regeneration or a feat of volunteer-led reforestation. I followed the tops over to the ski area, which wasn't part of the partnership, and from this distance I could just make out the roof of the Ptarmigan restaurant at the top of the out-of-service funicular railway. I handed the binoculars back to Jeremy.

'This is the forest expansion aspiration that we have. At the moment, we have approximately 130 square kilometres of forest in the project area. We know from mapping the soils and altitude that we could get another 130 square kilometres. That's vast in UK terms.'

I was still lost.

'These trees you're seeing are at about 750 to 800 metres above sea level.'

That was the significance. They were able to demonstrate in the project area that regeneration was happening naturally at high altitudes. There were montane willows growing at around 950 metres above sea level. That was impressive. That was equivalent to the summit of a Munro, where I certainly didn't picture tree cover. I guessed these montane species were usually quite small and scrubby, like the dwarf birch.

Another of Cairngorms Connect's projects had been to reintroduce 3,000 willow saplings into the Loch A'an basin. This rare species of downy willow already existed in areas of the Cairngorms, particularly on cliff edges inaccessible to browsing animals. Being able to withstand low temperatures and high winds made the species particularly suited to such a high altitude habitat in the Cairngorms.

The gravel track narrowed, and I walked behind Jeremy down the tree-covered hillside to the bottom of the pass. It gave me a sense of what a Caledonian pinewood remnant was like, with its old trees and deadwood. We stepped over tree roots, down stone steps and over narrow waterways. As we moved through the understorey, Jeremy pointed out the different species that surrounded us, as if making an inventory. Juniper, heather, blueberry, honeysuckle, dog's mercury. The latter was an ancient woodland indicator species, on account of its slow growth. I was amazed that so many different species were

129

growing in such close proximity to the path. It was like walking through a botanical garden.

'People often think of pinewoods as just being pine, but really 15 to 20 per cent, possibly more, would originally have been other species,' Jeremy explained. On the slopes around us, he showed me the abundance of juniper, birch, alder and willow, and I remembered Peter telling me how rare juniper was.

Cairngorms Connect didn't tend to focus on single-species management, but some individuals within the partnership did. Twinflower, which Jeremy had mentioned earlier, was a species that was new to me, and so far on our walk, Jeremy hadn't pointed it out. He told me it was a tiny flower with a double bell and tendrils that ran through the forest floor. There was a programme running in the partnership to connect patches of twinflower because they were not cross pollinating, which meant they weren't producing seed or diversifying genetically.

Jeremy also talked about the partnership's work around capercaillie, the world's largest grouse. In 2021, the Cairngorms Connect area held 55 per cent of the overall capercaillie population in Scotland. Just four years earlier, it had been 50 per cent. Some of the partners were focused on creating habitats for Capercaillie; he had already described how restructuring and thinning out the plantations could hugely benefit capercaillie. They were also trialling how to manage the understorey in some areas. He admitted that some of this work was trial and error. With other species, there might be five key things you could do to make a habitat more supportive. With capercaillie, Jeremy explained, it was much more complicated.

'After decades of work to try to crack the issue, capercaillie are still in decline, but in this area we've at least still got them.'

I'd been aware of how endangered the capercaillie was my

whole life. Their chances of survival never seemed to improve, much like the wildcat, which was now technically extinct. I'd felt some trepidation about raising the subject of the capercaillie, so Jeremy's willingness to talk about it was a relief. I knew that the partnership was facing difficulties, particularly in areas where habitat had been subject to significant deer culling. The reduction in browsing by deer meant that the habitat's understorey grew taller, and that meant young capercaillie couldn't escape the wet vegetation to dry out. As a result, many died of hypothermia in the wet field layer. Permission was being sought to flatten the understorey in an area that was under designation, to try to resolve the issue.

It was an upsetting story when I first heard about it. But in a sense it was unsurprising. Our landscapes are made up of layers of human intervention for the management of one species or another, each aiming to undo the mistakes we've made in the past or trying to improve things for the future, but always at a cost to non-human species.

We met a family climbing up the path towards us. The kids clambered up the steps, placing flat palms on the trunks of the pines for support. We stepped out of their path as Jeremy hollered a friendly and emphatic 'Hi folks' as if he were a holiday rep and the family were heading back from the lido. The mother, commenting on the fine weather, said in a familiar Central Belt accent, 'Where in the world are we!?'

'Scotland!' responded Jeremy emphatically. I found myself cringing a little at the promotional feel of the encounter.

We continued to follow the steep narrow path down into the pass, and in some parts I was having to crouch and lower myself down to the next stone slab, all the while trying to keep up with Jeremy so I could catch what he was saying. I went quiet as I focused on my feet, and we encountered another group who had stepped to the side for us. Jeremy noticed the steepness of the steps and took a moment to check in on me. Like the kids earlier, I placed my palms on the ancient pines to steady myself as I clambered down. Jeremy came to a stop as the understorey opened up around us and we reached the bottom of the pass. He'd just seen something, and he listened to confirm his sighting. It was a willow warbler. Jeremy pointed out the little family of birds moving in and out of a birch tree.

I was so busy watching my feet that I couldn't fully take in my surroundings. I thought back to Sandra who had encouraged me to find a spot in nature and sit still. I would have loved to have done that at this moment.

We eventually reached An Lochan Uaine, the Green Loch. It sat like a little basin on Sgòr an Lochain Uaine, surrounded by Scots pines. Directly across the water from us was a scree-covered hillside that slipped into the lochan. Some visitors had gone for a paddle. The water, instead of being peat coloured as you'd expect, was a very inviting aquamarine or green, hence its name. Expecting a scientific answer, I asked Jeremy what made the water that colour.

'It's where the fairies wash their clothes of course.'

In truth, it was thought that perhaps the surrounding trees gave the lochan its colour, either that or it was minerals from the surrounding rocks. I'd heard there were leeches in the water, though Jeremy was unsure as to whether this was true. He did, however, notice the warning signs for blue-green algae blooms. We set off again toward the Ryvoan bothy. The forest had begun to thin, and it revealed another face of Meall a' Bhuachaille, which rose abruptly from the peatland.

I picked this moment to be more candid with Jeremy about my concerns around the rewilding and ecological restoration movement in Scotland. I told him I couldn't shake my discomfort at the super-rich making decisions about land, even if those decisions were seen to benefit biodiversity.

'Is your question about why they are entitled to make those decisions?'

'I think it's more about why they are doing it,' I replied.

This was obviously not the first time Jeremy had had to speak on behalf of landowners.

'The first thing is, there is a land-ownership pattern in Scotland that lots of folk will have views about. That pattern exists in Cairngorms Connect, but also with the sporting estates and grouse-moor estates. That land ownership pattern is common irrespective of the land management that overlies that. Then it comes down to these owners being in a position to manage the land for restoration. That's the approach they've decided to take, and for some of them, it's absolutely a personal belief that it's the right thing to do.'

Jeremy highlighted that there were a lot of incentives for land managers to carry out restoration. The Scottish Government had grants in place for the creation of woodland and peatland restoration.

'I don't think some of the wealthy landowners are at all motivated by that money. They'll use it, but they're motivated by their own objectives.'

But it wasn't solely about the objectives or desires of wealthy landowners: there was the expectation that, across Scotland, land managers and landowners would seriously consult with and consider a community's views on decisions about land management. The RSPB, Forestry and Land Scotland and NatureScot were all bound into that approach, Jeremy told me, with Wildland moving in that direction.

'The final thing is, if you are a wealthy landowner, you can deliver things that aren't just things that you like but are also a benefit to people.' Jeremy reeled off not just the ecosystem benefits of what the partnership was doing, but also the numerous recreational and tourist benefits. In my naivety, I'd never really considered that wealthy landowners tended to focus on delivering the things that they were interested in, whether that be ecological restoration or hunting game. I'd always assumed that sporting estates were such because it meant they were economically viable, not because it was something the landowner genuinely liked and had an interest in. Realising that over half of Scotland's land, more according to some reports, was managed for the activities of a traditional sporting estate largely because of landowners' interests and hobbies raised my blood pressure.

Jeremy continued. 'Some people like to portray ecological restoration as de-peopling, but if you want to control deer without lynx or wolves, you need people.'

We reached a fork in the path and a sign that asked that dogs be kept on a lead, which Jeremy used to illustrate his point. 'If you have seasonal signs, you've got to pay someone to design them, and another to put them up. If you want to improve a track, you've got to have people. If you want to show wildlife, you've got to employ people.'

And so on. He listed a whole host of temporary and seasonal rural jobs, some that required qualifications, some that required a high level of physical ability and expertise. I thought of the redundancies and evictions on 'green estates' that seemed to demonstrate a reduction in employment. I also thought about all the other things required for someone to carry out these jobs: the ability to drive, access to a vehicle and the ability to be based locally – for some, owing to lack of housing, this had to be as far away as Inverness. I thought of the barriers to these roles: sexism, classism, ableism, ageism, racism. I thought of the amount of volunteering you were expected to do before working for many conservation charities, and of those who couldn't afford to volunteer.

It seemed Jeremy was reading my mind, as he told me that the partnership was raising funds for at least three apprenticeship or traineeship schemes. Without any prompting from me, he acknowledged that all the people running the partnership were white men in their fifties or so. He was upfront too about there being no diversity at the partnership's board level, meaning there was no diversity in the decision-making processes, and that seriously concerned the partnership. Jeremy discussed how they were going to rectify this – by connecting with diverse communities, utilising a bottom-up decision-making process and even reaching out into the world of social-media influencers. Ryvoan bothy came into view. It seemed smaller than I remembered from my school days. A few visitors were sitting outside, eating their lunch. Others were packing up and getting ready to tackle the track up and over Meall a' Bhuachaille. My eyes followed the track up and up, and I was glad we weren't attempting it in this heat.

Jeremy directed my attention out across the open ground towards the expanding forest and its natural tree regeneration. We were surrounded by young rowan trees. Further away, across the moor, was a collection of birch and aspen which had been planted to create a seed source for future regeneration. I remembered how rare aspen had been at one time from my previous conversation with Peter. The combination of low deer numbers, an established seed source and a moorland bird population had created, in ecological terms, a positive feedback loop. In short, the birds ate the rowan berries then nested overnight in the heather, where they pooped out the seeds of the berries. The seeds germinated in the spring, and the high number of saplings meant they stood a better chance against the already low number of browsing deer. Those saplings then grew up to create more seed source, and eventually more saplings, and the loop continued.

The partnership's long-term thinking and 200-year vision made Cairngorms Connect unique. I had assumed the 200 years were a PR hook, a way to differentiate one ecological restoration project from other rewilding initiatives, or as a means to assert the partnership's legitimacy in a context where the very nature of land ownership was evolving. I asked Jeremy more about this, and he told me that the 200-year vision had been scientifically calculated as the length of time it would take for tree regeneration in the area to reach the higher slopes of the hills. He went into some detail about the research project the partnership had embarked on to ascertain a timescale. It involved measuring how far the seeds carried from a mother tree, how many of those seeds were viable, the browsing behaviours of other species and the age an established tree started to make seed. Using this data, the partnership was able to almost pace out across the moor in decades the length of the time it would take to achieve their restoration vision. The 200-year vision also applied to the peatland, but realistically this restoration process would be much slower because of its high altitude.

We began the walk back toward An Lochan Uaine, and it was a relief when we eventually reached the cooler tree cover – an apt reminder of just how important trees are in a climate crisis. It didn't escape me that there was a connection between the partnership's 200-year vision and the indigenous Seventh Generation Principle that Dr Sandra Engstrom had talked about. I asked Jeremy if he'd come across the concept before, and I was surprised to learn that he hadn't. I thought that it might have been another reason for the 200-year vision. We roughly added up what we thought a generation was, 30 years or thereabouts, and it tantalisingly aligned with the partnership's timescale. I could see Jeremy's mind ticking over with ways this might inform their community engagement, and I was happy to have done my own little bit of cross-pollination of ideas.

Jeremy's focus shifted when he saw a couple headed towards us with a dog, but this time there was no wide smile or bright hello from him. Instead, he stopped and politely but firmly asked the couple to put their dog on the lead. It was the middle of the capercaillie breeding season, he added. The couple was apologetic. Jeremy wasn't in a Cairngorms ranger polo shirt, so it wasn't clear to any passers-by who he was or why he might have the authority to call them out. But here he was, regardless, advocating on behalf of the park's endangered species. This happened repeatedly on our walk back towards Glenmore, and I became fascinated with the different responses to Jeremy's polite but firm requests. Some were apathetic, others insisted that their dog was under control, and others ignored him altogether. Jeremy continued, undeterred.

The younger trees gave way to more mature woodland with its remnants of ancient forest. We passed An Lochan Uaine again, and a few more outdoor swimmers were braving the leeches and algae blooms. The series of dog-owner encounters had meant that we'd lost the thread of our original conversation, so I reverted to my usual topic of choice, ecological grief.

I asked if Jeremy thought there was room within ecological restoration to hold a space for grief and mourning. I could see his mind whirring again. He told me that, as a partnership, they'd struggled to find a framework to facilitate community engagement that wasn't just focused on consultation. I suggested they might consider an emotional, rather than only physical, offering.

Jeremy admitted that he was uncomfortable about the burden his generation had left my generation and his children's generation. 'And I've been someone who's been involved all my life in ecological restoration. So I am pretty aware, and I've done a lot, and yet I'm really embarrassed.'

I'd never asked my own family about this, or even spent time interrogating it myself. I assumed too that my family on the estate in Drumochter never considered the legacy of their working practices on the land. However, I'm sure they observed changes in vegetation, increased grouse and deer numbers, fewer saplings each spring.

*

The idea of connection, spatial and temporal, ran through every aspect of Cairngorms Connect's objectives: connecting habitats, connecting species and connecting people to those habitats and species. How could people understand or appreciate the benefits of the partnership's work if they didn't believe they directly benefitted from it? Jeremy suggested thinking about the very individualistic question 'What do *I* get out of it?' So I did. I wasn't local to the Cairngorms area anymore, so I couldn't visit as much as I'd like. Clearly, many people benefitted from the tranquil walks, the clean lochs to swim in, jobs or careers within the local economy, or even just the confidence that their riverside caravan wouldn't be washed away. But how did I benefit personally? I thought long and hard about this, and I came to the realisation that I experienced a significant amount of place attachment to the Cairngorms. Its peaks, lochs, and forests were interwoven with my family history and childhood. Now, because of Cairngorms Connect, I had reassurance that this place wouldn't be destroyed. It would be enhanced. And there were very few places in the world I could say that about with such confidence. This, I recognised, was an incredible salve.

The roof of the Glenmore Centre came into view, signalling the end of our walk. Jeremy felt something on one of his calves. He leaned down and batted away a persistent cleg, examining his leg. It had got him. A rivulet of warm blood ran down towards his boot. I had known shorts were a bad idea.

10

The Stalk, Part Three

The Argo comes to a stop in the fresh snow line of Tom an Eòin, and as soon as the diesel engine is turned off an astonishing silence settles around us. Allan turns to me and asks what's in my backpack. 'Layers,' I reply.

He suggests that I leave it behind in the Argo, and, seeing the hesitation on my face, explains that it could be a hindrance. 'It'll be noisy, rubbing against your coat.'

I'm mortified. Despite my preparations, I've failed to account for one of the most important tools in a stalker's arsenal: the ability to move silently, and I've inadvertently layered up with some of the noisiest fabrics possible. My gaiters will swish-swoosh with every step, and my coat, an oversized puffy jacket, although cosy, is not inconspicuous. I've deliberately worn dark colours, thinking this might help me blend into the hill, but I haven't accounted for the brilliant white of the first snow. We are in the snow line, and any deer that happen to look up would of course be suspicious of the unusual puffy dark beacon on the hill. Allan and Ethan jump out of the Argo as I grab an extra layer from the backpack and put it on, in part to prove my earlier claim about its contents, but also to make it appear I'm more prepared than I feel. I quickly put my top layers back on and jump out of the Argo to join them, leaving behind my audio recorder, water, snacks and my inhaler. It's fine, I think, we'll be back to have lunch in a couple of hours.

Allan's been standing in quiet discussion with Ethan, coming up with a strategy for the stalk. After a few moments, he brings a pair of binoculars up to his face. The snow is maybe a few inches deep, not enough to obscure the terrain under foot, but definitely enough to be an impediment. I take a deep lungful of familiar Highland air, and as I slowly, quietly, exhale, I find myself in awe. Corrour is as beautiful as I'd hoped it would be, and I feel genuinely enraptured. I look back down to the train station at the foot of the mountain and see the now tiny railway sign. The winter sky is a strange mix of bright early morning light and heavy low cloud. The rising sun makes Loch Ossian glimmer, creating a golden layer of water and sky beneath a heavy plateau of stratocumulus clouds. It looks like a drone shot from a VisitScotland promotional video, perpetuating the illusion of vast swathes of 'wilderness' and 'uninhabited' landscapes.

The air is crisp with a very light breeze, perfect conditions for a stalk, I think to myself.

'The conditions aren't ideal,' Allan says. He casually plucks some grass, tosses it into the air and watches it drift back to the ground. He's confirming the strength and direction of the breeze, and he seems slightly displeased. It's enough to put us at a disadvantage, as any herd on this side of the mountain will quickly be alerted to our presence. He points down into the glen at a small herd of deer he's seen through his binoculars and suggests we try to get closer. A little shiver of dread runs through me. My binoculars are back in the Argo in my backpack, and I can't see the deer. We set off in single file, with Allan leading, me in the middle and Ethan behind us with the rifle slung over his shoulder. Allan's not really walking, more gliding, and I'm scrambling my way along the hill face behind him. I clutch onto clumps of heather and whatever else is around me, negotiating my way through snow and thick vege-tation, sometimes walking sideways to keep my weight against the hill and avoid sliding down its face. Eventually Allan stops and crouches, brings his binoculars up to his face and signals for us to crouch and be quiet. I use this moment to catch my breath. The cold air makes my lungs burn. I look down into the glen, squinting my eyes. I still can't see the deer. I relax my focus and hope to see something move in my peripheral vision, like I used to do in the car at Drumochter. But nothing.

It dawns on me that we've started the stalk. How did that happen? I wasn't expecting a fanfare or a starting pistol, but I did expect a more obvious cue somehow. Apparently the herd has moved on, and Allan effortlessly makes his way back towards us. He tells us that we'll need to move on to the other face of the hill because of the breeze. We can't get close enough on this face without alerting the herd. On the other side of the hill we'll mostly be upwind. I get the sense that this means something else altogether, but I have no idea what.

We follow Allan up the slope, onto the plateau and over to the southern side of the hill. The vegetation here is very different: there's no heather, only scrubby grasses and plants. Allan stops to carry out another assessment. He plucks some grass again and watches it fall. There's much less of a breeze here. He looks up and says, 'We're going to have to wait here a bit . . . the ravens.' He indicates an unkindness of ravens circling above us.

'Will the ravens alert the deer to our presence?' I ask.

'Not quite,' Allan says, a smile crossing his face. Both the deer and the ravens associate the noise of the Argo with people. The ravens currently associate it with food too, and they don't want the deer to come to associate it with the sound of the rifle. So we have to wait a while before doing the stalk in earnest, to give the herd a chance to settle as the ravens disperse.

In the meantime, we quietly chat, and Allan orientates me. Northwest of where we're standing is Loch Treig; Ben Nevis is to our west, and in the southwest, beyond the Blackwater reservoir, is Buachaille Etive Mòr, one of Scotland's iconic mountains. Allan stops abruptly as we hear an animal call. He listens intently, and there's a small squeak.

'White hare,' Allan confirms. I feel the rapture grow again like a wave.

The ravens have moved on, and we begin the stalk properly this time. At first we move southwest through the snow line, away from the Argo. We're back in single file, and Allan stays some metres ahead of us. He regularly moves downhill towards the edge of the snow line, where he crouches and encourages us to join him. I keep as quiet as I can. He lies on his stomach, and I join him and keek over a rock at the moor below us. It's a patchwork of russets, browns and peat. From this height, I find my depth perception distorted, and it's difficult to distinguish one russet mound from another. Allan hands me his binoculars and tells me there's a herd. I look through them hoping to see something, anything, but all I can see are the russet mounds in more detail. I take the binoculars away from my face and search for some kind of landmark, finding only a peat hag. I look back through the binoculars, seeking out my hag. Nothing. I can't find it. Well, this doesn't bode well, I think. If I can't see a peat hag through an expensive pair of binoculars, how am I supposed to see a deer through the sight of a rifle? Allan asks if I can see the herd.

'Yup,' I lie, still keeping up the pretence that – what? I'm good at this? Ethan joins us and has a look too, and of course he can see them. Allan concludes that we can't get close enough to this herd, so we back away from the ledge, quietly and slowly.

There's an old superstition that if you hunt a deer quickly and easily, your life will be short, but if it takes longer and is more difficult, you will live a long life. At this rate I'm going to outlive a lot of people.

The next few hours follow the same pattern. We creep down the hill, then creep up the hill, then down the hill, then up the hill. Eventually I'm exhausted and stop going downhill with Allan altogether in a bid to save some of my energy. I don't need my inhaler, but the exertion and cold air is still making it painful to breathe, and I really need a drink to try to relax my throat and warm it up. I sit and do some ujjayi breathing I've learned from yoga classes to create some heat. As I focus on my breath, I watch Allan work. It's clear how well he knows the topography of this landscape – every overhang, mound and fissure. He slowly works his way across hill from one vantage point to the next, ensuring that we never alert the herd. He often stops and crouches, bringing his binoculars up to his face. He confirms the strength and direction of the wind, perhaps when a deer abruptly stops its grazing or glances in his direction. He's not just looking for a hind. He's also assessing the tension within the herd, in their bodies, to see if they're alert or at ease. If alert, he needs to understand whether the perceived threat is us. If it is, we back off. If it's not us, we have to steer clear of the same threat. Not only do the deer need to be at ease, but they need to be within range, which in this instance means within a distance of 100 metres. So the stalk becomes a delicate dance between proximity and tension. However, it's only really months after the stalk that I come to understand these nuances.

I fish my phone out of my pocket. It's 1 p.m. I could really do with going back to the Argo and having a hot drink and some lunch, but I don't even consider asking if we can stop. There's a pressure building to get this done and over with, the feeling that if we stop now, we'll lose the momentum of the stalk, and all of our efforts will have been for naught. I decided to ignore the exhaustion and the pain in my lungs and keep going. I look down at Allan who's now crouched behind a rock some metres below me. Ethan's with him, and I look past them to the moor. I'm still unable to distinguish a herd from the overwhelming russet. Allan makes a gesture for me to join them, but on my stomach, quietly crawling through the snow down the hill, commando style. This change in approach must mean that the stakes are higher. Allan must have spotted a herd, and, not only this, he must be satisfied that the conditions mean I have a higher chance of successfully taking the shot. Another shiver of dread runs through me.

Heart pounding, I quietly slide down to Allan's side as Ethan makes some space and observes through binoculars. Allan delicately sets up the tripod for the rifle and checks the scope. He invites me up to the rifle, and I slide towards it, still on my stomach. I'm trembling, but it could just be the cold. I take deep breaths and try to steady myself. I put my eye up to the scope, and Allan comes closer and describes in hushed tones what to look for in the sight.

'You should be able to see a group of four hinds, each facing right. They're feeding.'

I can't see them, and I panic, I desperately search the landscape framed in the scope. Russet. All I see are mounds of russet. I lift my face away and look down to the moor. Again, I try to find a landmark. Back to the scope now. Careful not to move the rifle too much, I search and search, but I can't see them. I have no sense of how small or large they should be, what tone of brown I'm looking for, what texture they might be against the grasses. Allan asks if I can see them. 'Not yet,' I reply, trying to stay calm.

'Come away from the scope,' he says. 'There's a small peat hag to the left of the herd with sphagnum moss on its upper ledge, can you see it?'

I can.

'Okay, look for that in the sights.' I bring my face back to the scope and try to find this new landmark. The green sphagnum should stand out against the overwhelming russet. I can feel the frustration making me tense up, and I focus on my breath again, exhaling slowly. I finally stumble across the sphagnum in the crosshairs and hold the position. I gently move the crosshairs to the right and see a hind.

'I see them,' I whisper.

Allan comes close again and guides me through the herd.

'Look for the one standing third from the left. She'll be more in the foreground than the others.'

I find her. This is the first hind I've seen all day. I watch her through the crosshairs as she browses her way slowly across the moor. She's perfectly camouflaged against the russet. At ease. Beautiful. A shiver of dread comes. This can't be right. I thought the cull focused on removing deer that were old, injured or sick.

She's none of those things. She looks young, smaller than the others, and healthy, most likely pregnant.

'She's young,' I say questioningly.

'She's in a good position for the shot,' Allan replies.

He's correct, she is. Her right flank is exposed to me, just like on the illustration on the poster back in the office. This is the moment when people can be divided into two groups:

those who will pull the trigger and those who won't. These are the brief seconds in which I've promised myself I'll have permission not to take the shot. I could simply let her walk out of the crosshairs, but the weight of expectation is bearing down on me. The hours and hours we've spent on the hill. The effort it's taken to set up a good shot. The larger objectives of the cull. I don't want to be on the hill anymore, but I don't feel like I have a choice. I centre her in the crosshairs then move from the top of her right leg down a third. I take a deep breath and exhale slowly. At the end of my breath, I force myself to keep my eye open and squeeze the trigger.

*

The superb sound of the gunshot reverberates around the hills, and for a split second I see her rise onto her hind legs, arching her back, with her two front legs out in front of her as she stumbles backwards. Then the recoil pushes my shoulder, and I lose her from the sight. I'm stunned and forget to eject the shell casing and reload. Allan takes over the rifle and reloads, but it's too late. The panicked herd is running across the moor, towards the Blackwater.

Terrified that I've only maimed her, I ask Allan if he thinks it was a clean shot.

'It was a great shot,' he tells me.

Relief rather than pride washes over me as I recall the hind's last moments in the sight. I try to make sense of what she did, of the shape she made. The shock of it, and the pain. I'd never considered what it would look like to shoot a hind. I go to stand up, but Allan stops me. 'Stay down. We need to wait so the herd doesn't see us.' As I settle again, I become aware that the tension has dissipated and the mood around me is different. It's not celebratory or jubilant, but neither is it sympathetic or mournful; it's just lighter. Stalker and ghillie have had another successful stalk, another hind to add to the cull count, another satisfied client. Except I'm quietly devastated.

As I wait amongst the mosses and heather, I spot the expelled bullet casing and pick it up. I turn it over in my hand. It's as plain as any I've seen, but it's now imbued with meaning. I close my hand around the casing. It's not a trophy but a kind of totem. In an instant, I know it will bring me back to this moment with the hind on the hill. I carefully slip it into my pocket.

Eventually, we get up. Allan instructs Ethan to go back to the Argo. I'd assumed we'd all be going back there, so I ask what we're doing now.

'I thought we could get another,' Allan suggests.

I look at him, surprised. 'Oh okay, yeah,' I say.

Allan slings the rifle over his shoulder, and Ethan makes off back up the hill to the Argo, but I don't move. I just stand there on the hill, freezing cold, hungry, soaking wet from the snow. Allan strikes out across the hill, and in a little voice only just loud enough to be heard I speak to his back.

'I've had enough now.'

11

Carving

Beavers of Bamff

Midsummer 2019. I was standing in a supermarket car park in the west end of Glasgow with my backpack and walking boots. I waited beside one of the few trees and observed the cars looping around the tiny car park as pedestrians negotiated their way to the train station, each committed to their own migratory routes and desire lines. This was the agreed meeting point for the small Glasgow-based contingent of artists and academics travelling to Bamff in Perthshire for a weekend residency. Residency colleague Scott, a composer, soon joined me in watching the cars. This was my first time on a residency with the organisers, David Overend and Jamie Lorimer, but Scott had been with them the previous year in Knepp, West Sussex, home to the high-profile rewilding project led by Isabella Tree and her husband Sir Charles Burrell. I had just finished reading Tree's book *Wilding* and was looking forward to stealing an opportunity to talk with people who had been there and experienced it.

For the Bamff residency, Jamie and David had brought together a small group of artists, geographers and academics to take part in a weekend workshop beguilingly titled Landscaping with Beavers. We were to be hosted by the owners of the estate, the Ramsays.

I had a sense of what to expect during the residency: lots of listening, talking, sharing of ideas, and observing Bamff's beaver family. I'd participated in many different types of residencies around the UK with artists from different disciplines, and I really enjoyed this kind of work. However, this was the first residency that had brought my practice as a theatre maker into a context of ecological restoration. I was hugely excited about seeing beavers in a habitat that they'd constructed.

There was one little concern at the back of my mind, though. Having seen the documentation from the residency at Knepp, I knew there was the chance I might be asked to pretend to be a beaver. Working in performance, I've been asked to imitate many different things over the years. I've spent hours trying to depict the lifecycle of a single-cell organism or contorting myself into the shape of inanimate objects. I draw the line, however, at pretending to be an animal.

David soon arrived to pick us up, and was quickly followed by Laura, another artist and academic. We were soon on the M8 headed toward Bamff Estate. Before the residency, I didn't know much about Bamff, and I was only aware of the Knapdale beavers – in 2009, four beavers had been released into Loch Coille Bharr in Knapdale, Lochgilphead, as part of a five-year reintroduction trial. I had no idea there had been private reintroductions in Scotland, too. The Bamff beavers had arrived in 2002 and were kept in a large enclosure. They eventually bred, creating the families that exist in Bamff today.

We were visiting the estate at a politically interesting time for both the Ramsays and the beavers. Just one month earlier, the Scottish Government had announced new beaver protection laws, recognising the beaver's status as a European Protected Species. Before this, any beaver, including the Knapdale beavers, found outside of captivity could be killed; now a licence was required.

The weather was bright and everything green as we snaked our way through some of the finest agricultural land in Perthshire. We eventually reached a fork in the road and branched off to the right past an inconspicuous sign that read *Bamff* in a friendly script typeface. David's driving slowed as everyone in the car looked out of the windows expectantly, hoping for a glimpse of something that could be interpreted as beaver activity. We gently bumped along the single-track road past a mix of plantation, woodland, rhododendrons and grazed fields. Bamff was still hosting some farmland at the time, and it served to demonstrate how rewilding land was a gradual process.

The main house emerged just as we passed a large pile of timber ready for the sawmill. Scott remarked on how busy the beavers must have been to create such a large log pile and the hush in the car immediately dissolved into laughter.

We arrived at the sixteenth-century house and were greeted by George, the youngest sibling in the Ramsay family. He looked at me quizzically for a moment and then exclaimed, 'We've met before.'

I froze, never quite sure how to react in these moments.

'The Edinburgh Fringe,' he confirmed with absolute certainty.

George and I had shared a venue and a dressing room at Summerhall in 2012. I came off stage everyday for a month to find George and his co-performers slathered in clay ready to perform their show. Of all the places I might bump into George again, I wouldn't have guessed an ecotourism estate in Perthshire. It was good to see him, but the likelihood of having to imitate a beaver seemed even stronger now.

We discovered, once everyone had arrived, that we'd all

made the same joke about the log pile. It turned out to be an effective little ice-breaker. Everyone introduced themselves, and we met Louise and Paul Ramsay along with other members of the Ramsay family, including their daughter Sophie, who would soon take over Bamff's rewilding project. We'd all been allocated rooms around Bamff House, but one lucky individual would be able to spend the evening in the Hideaway, an off-grid hut situated at the edge of an active beaver pond. I opted to stay in the house, and soon found myself tucked away in a corner of the building. The window looked out onto a recently grazed field with a burn running through it. In the exterior of the window frame lived some honeybees, and their early morning hum proved to be a reassuring sound to wake up to.

Over dinner we discussed rewilding and shared our enthusiasm for the reintroduction of beavers and the recent change in law. The dining room felt grand, with candelabras on the table, and silverware. I have to admit that on entering the main house, I had felt my behaviour change. I instinctively showed deference not only to our hosts, but also to the objects and furniture around us. The walls of the dining room were adorned with portraits of the Ramsays' ancestors. At one point, we compared George's face to one of the portraits. He was the spitting image of a gentleman in military attire, although George couldn't see the resemblance. The estate had been in the family for centuries, and Bamff house felt heavy with the legacy of each generation.

After dinner, and with plenty of time before sunset, we met Paul outside for our first walk around the estate. I was quietly beside myself with excitement, having never seen beavers nor been in their habitat. We quietly approached the ponds. There was no sign of the beavers as we passed their main pond – the crepuscular mammals weren't yet ready to venture out of their lodge. Paul guided us first around the old beaver pond. In front of us was a wetland that had been engineered by the beavers. Once a Victorian curling pond, the beavers' interventions had changed or restored it to a wetland. It was surrounded by what used to be a pine forest, but the beavers had felled much of that for dam building. In the wetlands were huge root plates of fallen trees and the stumps of dead pines sticking up over a metre out of the wet ground, their tips chiselled to a point. Some pines were in a state of collapse, their canopies now dipping into the water. Some had fallen on top of the wire deer fences. Paul remarked how the fence got in the way of the beaver's work. It looked chaotic and messy, as though some kind of environmental disaster had occurred. It was strange to realise that we were standing in a habitat that was being mostly managed by a non-human species. I held this thought as we left the old pond and made our way through the mature woodland over to the series of dams. I stared down at the ground, looking for field signs of other species, and occasionally looked up in the hope of spotting a red squirrel. The evening midsummer light illuminated the finest strands of spider web in the lush woodland understorey. It felt as though we were being watched by hundreds of sets of eyes, arthropodan, avian and mammalian. This broadleaf wood was alive and thriving.

We reached the lower part of the burn. The bank was littered with curls and discarded chunks of wood, strips of bark and wood chippings. Paul directed our attention to an older beaver dam, which had recently been repaired by the animals after some bad weather. Paul explained that the beavers would usually use the same materials and construct the dams in the same way each time. This dam was a little unusual, however: in the very middle, sitting on top of all the layers of wood and vegetation like a paper weight was a single white rock the size of a fist. Paul joked that it had been placed there by a beaver because of its aesthetic quality rather than its functionality. Across the burn from us was a derelict outbuilding which looked to be in the middle of a renovation. George told us that this was his project, but he had to pause work on it. Just as he was about to explain why, a flash of white darted out from an unglazed window opening.

'Barn owls,' he said. 'I can't work on it right now because barn owls are nesting there.' I was delighted to see a barn owl outside of captivity, and was struck by how committed the Ramsays were to prioritising the needs of the environment with their slow and sensitive approach to developments on the estate.

We continued to quietly make our way up the burbling burn past several dams. Along the banks for the burn, Paul pointed out areas of trampled grass where the beavers played and sites of abandoned felling projects. We reached the final dam. Behind it sat the largest and darkest pool, which was home to the beaver family. We lined ourselves up along the narrow track that ran adjacent to the pond and watched for any movement in the dense wall of rhododendrons that obscured the beavers' lodge. There was a large piece of deadwood lying half submerged in the middle of the pond. It served as a useful fortification that shielded the beavers as they emerged from the water. I wondered if the beavers knew we were there, whether they felt they were being watched. Paul reacted to an almost imperceptible sound, a small splosh. He pointed to somewhere behind the deadwood, and we all strained to see what it was. A beaver. At first it was difficult to distinguish its shape or colour from the deadwood and the darkness of the pond. The water gently rippled and gave up the beaver's position as it quietly swam, snout in the air, towards the adjacent bank. For the next 30 minutes, we watched in awe as an adult and a kit ate on the bank, lolled in the pond and slowly warmed up for an evening of bark stripping, dam maintenance and maybe even tree felling. I tried to comprehend the enormity of what I was witnessing: the reintroduction of a keystone species that had been missing from Scotland's landscapes for 400 years.

The contention round the reintroduction of beavers to Scotland stems from their status as ecosystem engineers. The beaver's instinct and ability to transform a landscape and its habitats through building dams, digging canals and creating deadwood provides multitudinous benefits for other species and supports greater biodiversity. Their dams and canals slow the flow of a water system, which can stabilise riverbanks and thereby benefit wetland species such as water voles. The deeper pools that are created naturally hold a greater volume of water, which would otherwise evaporate or disappear at different times of year, impacting on species including invertebrates and amphibians that depend on these habitats. The creation of wetlands by beavers helps the human species too: the pooling and slowing of water flow helps improve the quality of water through natural filtration and can act as a form of natural flood management because the land has already been 'engineered' by the beavers to hold more water, whether that be a wetland or a series of pools in waterways.

It's these wetlands, however, that come into direct conflict with anthropocentric forms of land use, notably agriculture. The damming of a burn on or near farmland can alter the irrigation hydrology necessary to support crop production. Homes and commercial properties are thought to be at risk in areas where beavers' dams may undermine flood defences. These risks are continually monitored and assessed to ensure appropriate mitigation. A Scottish Government Consultation Analysis from 2018 on the reintroduction of beavers showed that stakeholders agreed that Scotland's beavers should receive strong protections, based on the ecosystem benefits they provided, but legitimate concerns were raised regarding the long-term impact of beavers on land and land use. In spring 2022, NatureScot announced its management framework for beavers in Scotland, which includes information on the newly announced translocation licence, which offers an alternative to lethal control. Some of Scotland's largest conservation organisations and ecological restoration advocates, including the Scottish Wildlife Trust, the John Muir Trust and Trees for Life championed the return of beavers to Scotland, which I think indicates a strong recognition that improving biodiversity has to be a priority in Scotland's landscapes.

*

Over the next two days, we spent much of our time responding to the environment at Bamff and each other's practices and work. It was at one of these sessions that I shared with a colleague my resistance to pretending to be an animal. They queried this, hoping to understand where the discomfort came from. Shortly after our conversation, this colleague shared a film of their work. An image of two people in beaver costumes came up on the screen. Mortified, I sank deep into my chair. Soon it was my turn to share something. I projected onto the wall an image of Edward Landseer's *The Monarch of the Glen* in all its romanticised Highland glory. However, in place of the stag was a very poorly Photoshopped beaver. The purpose of the image, I told the group, was to reflect on our own experience of cultural speciesism. I asked them to consider what it would mean for another species to be Scotland's unofficial emblem. I was interested in whether our attitudes to beavers would have been shaped differently over the last few centuries. How might Scotland's landscapes have been impacted if they were managed to accommodate beavers instead of deer? I wondered what the landscape would look like, what the impact would be on biodiversity, and on us. Perhaps our towns and cities would have been established elsewhere, with the urban sprawl growing in alternative directions. Our roads and infrastructure might have been built away from beaver wetlands. Perhaps the way we engaged with land, and our relationship with nature, and with ourselves, would have been completely different.

As geographers, anthropologists, researchers and artists, we discussed the issues around an inherently anthropological relationship with any species and, ironically perhaps, whether you can ever create a truly collaborative artistic multi-species interaction. Over the weekend, we explored this question and created some really beautiful, playful interactions within the beavers' habitat, mainly at the edge of the burn. I participated in a bit of dam-building, which Paul assessed on behalf of the beavers. We had of course not met their specifications, but Paul assured us that they would be appreciative of the materials we'd gathered for them. On the penultimate day, we'd made our way out once again to the beaver pond. It was early afternoon, so we were unlikely to disrupt them. We had gathered at the Hideaway to have the next task explained to us: we were to experience the environment as if we were beavers. My worst fear had been realised. I quickly shuffled off into the woodland. Reluctant to get on all fours, I decided to take off my glasses and sit for a while taking in the sounds and smells of the forest. Much like myself, beavers have bad eyesight. The blurry woodland shifted and moved around me. The tree canopy was disturbed by the wind, or perhaps a red squirrel. I heard the occasional twig snap and imagined it to be an approaching predator or deer. I made my way across the understorey and took refuge under a large mature tree. At its base, I noticed a collection of bones, and I quickly left the feeding ground. I walked through the damp bracken and came across a narrow track beneath the ferns that had likely been made by some other species, perhaps deer. I followed it, and it eventually led me to the safety of the old beaver pond. I sat at the edge of the woods and looked out across the wetland. With my senses heightened, I could hear something walking behind me. I put on my glasses. George was on the other side of the trees, waving. I had lost track of time, so I quickly headed back to the Hideaway. There, the group had gathered to share their experiences. Some had found and even tried what might be a delicious food source to a beaver. Others had gone for a swim in the dark pools. I told them what I had done, and I felt pleased to have found some way of relating to the beaver.

We headed back to the house to enjoy our last dinner together. As the sun set, some people decided to go back to the pond to see the beavers one last time. I was instead content simply to know they were there, preparing for another evening of ecological restoration.

Louise of Bamff

Eighteen months later, I contacted Louise Ramsay again. I wanted to talk to her about an issue she'd raised during a panel discussion at the Big Picture Conference in 2019 – the challenges of passing down rewilded land to the next generation. I remembered seeing a lot of nodding across the audience; this seemed to be something many in the room had considered too. Little did I realise that our conversation would reframe my understanding of rewilding and the actions of many landowners across Scotland.

The point Louise had raised at the conference, she told me, was motivated by a warning they had received that rewilded land could not qualify for agricultural relief. As it turned out, this was actually a misunderstanding related to the common misconception that rewilded land is the same as neglected or abandoned land. However, because the Ramsays practised conservation grazing, Bamff was still eligible for agricultural relief from the Scottish Executive Environment Rural Affairs Department. Louise went on to share that they knew they were taking a risk by continuing to rewild the land in favour of industrial farming. This choice could have all sorts of financial implications in the years to come – less stability, less income, and the estate could face financial collapse. Many landowners who would like to rewild areas of their land may not do so, concerned that the Scottish Government won't provide any support. Yet despite the uncertainty, Bamff had fully committed to rewilding. They wanted to be trailblazers. Their private reintroduction of the beavers seventeen years before the protection order was testament to that. And if the estate were to be sold off, then at least it would be sold as a nature reserve.

Louise explained how their desire to be genuine stewards of Bamff meant managing the estate for nature. If they were to run the estate based on maximising inheritance and profit, they would be doing everything wrong for the environmental management of the land. And if the only way they could pass the estate on to their children was by doing things they didn't want to do, then what was the point? They would be passing down a badly managed estate to the next generation.

In discussing the financial differences between owning an estate tourism business and an estate with tenanted properties, I saw the ways in which ecotourism could be used as a form of greenwashing. An estate might extol the virtues of its ecological restoration efforts to entice 'ecotourists' into profitable, newly renovated holiday accommodation – estate buildings from which local tenants had been evicted. Thinking about this, I felt uncomfortable playing the role of ecotourist myself, although at Bamff I'd seen how the Ramsays were actively renovating derelict estate buildings or using purpose-built accommodation such as the hideaway or yurts.

I told Louise about the hind stalk. I had assumed that, as a landowner, she was probably quite into shooting, but I was wrong.

'I don't want to suggest that killing animals is a good thing. We stopped shooting here about six years ago,' she told me. 'Shooting or blood sports, depending on your perspective, are very tied up with our class system.'

I thought about what the differing nuances between shooting and blood sports might be. Perhaps it was down to intention – the necessity of a deer cull compared to the pleasure of shooting grouse, say.

'I don't like it on the whole,' Louise continued. 'It's both rather sexist and classist, additional reasons for it not to chime very well with the modern era. As society develops in a more meritocratic way, there's something out of tune about it. When we did have a shoot here, only our friends would come. I would cook, and Paul would get the drinks. You get beer for the beaters and wine for the alphas. There's something embarrassing about them and us.'

I had never heard a landowner express this concern before, let alone do something about it. The Ramsays were choosing to retire a Highland estate trope in the name of progression, and this has continued with their Wildland Bamff project, led by Sophie Ramsay, and which will allow the land to become self-willed and self-regenerating in order to provide dynamic habitats for a greater diversity of species.

I remembered that on an edge of the estate, where the burn flows onto neighbours' land, was a tunnel, which the beavers would be able to leave through should they wish to. I asked Louise about the challenges they faced in protecting their beaver families. I was surprised to hear that they don't do anything to protect them.

'Actually, at Bamff, we couldn't protect them, and I don't think we need to, because on the whole people don't come onto your land and kill animals. But we are aware that if the beavers leave Bamff and go onto agricultural ground, they are at risk, and we're campaigning against current government policy to get it changed, so the environment is less dangerous for beavers: more mitigation, more compromise, more relocation, less shooting.'

The 2019 protection order meant that beavers could still be killed, under licence. In the subsequent year, 87 beavers, or one fifth of the total population, were shot across Scotland. In response, Bamff created an art action in collaboration with Extinction Rebellion Scotland and the Scottish Wild Beaver Group. They brought together an exhibition of artistic responses to memorialise the loss of each of the 87 beavers, transforming them into grievable entities, and offered a space to mourn.

Fortunately, since my conversation with Louise, the Scottish Government has granted their first 'edge of range' translocation licence to support the expansion of beaver populations. Any dispersing beavers, including any Bamff beavers, can now be safely trapped and relocated to a more suitable habitat, away from areas of conflicted land use.

Louise shared the ways in which the Ramsays' lives had

been immeasurably changed for the better since the arrival of the beavers. She admitted that they had no idea what an immense impact the beavers would have on them and the land. They've seen a rise in visitors, through the tourism side of the business, and with engagement through events like the Landscaping with Beavers residency. They found the estate opened up socially and commercially. It even brought Sophie Ramsay back home to take on the estate, making it her life's work with the new rewilding programme. I asked Louise if she thought Sophie being a female landowner would challenge sexist stereotypes. Louise found the environmental world to be far less sexist than the landowning and gamekeeping world, though she was aware of more daughters taking on land, and the acceptance that women could do the same things as men was at least percolating through to the farming and landowning world.

Similar to my own experience, Louise's commitment to the environmental world had been cemented after she came across a book. Whereas for me it was *Feral*, for her it was *High Tide* by Mark Lynas. But she didn't get really involved in campaigning until it was suggested that the trial beavers of the Tay should be killed.

'Paul and I looked at each other and agreed, we're not having this, are we? And I started a campaign, Save the Free Beavers of the Tay. That eventually became the Scottish Wild Beaver Group. We've had some successes and some failures. We also joined the Scottish Rewilding Alliance, and we're part of that bigger movement.'

I noticed that the hard feeling of grief in my stomach had softened, and I asked Louise about how ecological grief manifested itself in her.

She confirmed what I already thought. 'I think I channel my

grief into anger,' she said, 'and then I channel my anger into action. I think that's my process. I can't really deal with the grief. But here is somewhere that I can do something positive for the environment, and in relation to climate change as well. I can do stuff on the ground which is constructive and positive. I can educate and excite people.'

She hadn't allowed herself to be consumed or paralysed by ecological grief, and she hadn't simply chosen to live with it either. She had made space for positive action – damming, pooling and slowing her grief through the impacts of her work at Bamff, and in so doing creating a rich and vital new landscape.

12

Retracing

Alladale

'What are you wanting from me?'

The question came before we'd even said hello properly. Innes MacNeill, Alladale's reserve manager, a tall, stubble-faced Highlander, strode around me in a wide arc towards a Land Rover, then turned to hear my answer. He softened when he saw my perturbed expression.

'I've had a few different people this week, and I can't keep track of who needs what.'

I quickly told him about my family connection to deer stalking and how I felt conflicted about rewilding.

'What do you need?'

'Your perspective.'

After years of following Alladale's rewilding journey, I was desperate to see the estate in person. Could it match up to the image I'd created in my head of a biodiverse utopia?

Innes seemed indifferent as he opened the passenger door of his Land Rover. I took a huge step up into the vehicle. The seat had been pushed right back for a much taller person, and I fell into it as I tried to pull the door closed behind me. It slammed, but I could see it hadn't shut fully. I slammed it again and again as Innes watched me until it finally clicked closed.

He put the Land Rover into gear, and we slowly drove through the deep gravel around the back of the lodge. Innes informed me that a journalist had been up from England the day before, also wanting to know more about the reserve.

'So what do you want? To see trees?' he asked, almost sarcastically.

'Show me what you'd normally show someone,' I replied, curious as to what the journalist had seen.

Innes stopped a little way past the lodge and into the glen. I could see some of the guest accommodation and Glen Alladale beyond. It was a dry day and only slightly overcast, so the tops of the hills were visible. In a field in front of us, one of Innes's estate workers was busy cutting the grass. Innes began delivering the Alladale fact sheet, describing the accommodation and the hydroelectric energy supply in front of us. I listened attentively and mentally ticked off the items on a typical rewilded estate: guest accommodation, renewable energy scheme, heather and scrub, meandering watercourse, natural regeneration, riparian planting, Scots pine, fences and so on.

I wasn't feeling my usual sense of awe or wonder, that biophilic joy. I wondered if it was because I'd seen an abundance of rewilded sites recently. Maybe it was simply the prospect of bumping along in a Land Rover for two to three hours. Whatever it was, I think Innes and I were reflecting each other's mood.

He continued in a monotone. 'We've planted 650,000 trees; they're behind a big fence. We've taken this approach to protect the habitat: it's short-term loss, long-term gain. Fences up, get the trees established, and in the future let the deer back in, and other various other wildlife. The view that we're seeing now – we all know it's not meant to look like this: it's meant to have more forest cover.' He pointed to some trees at a distance in the scree up on the hillside. They'd been core-bored and were estimated to be about 470 years old.

'I have theories. I'm not a scientist, I'm not an ecologist, but we've planted trees in this glen and put something back, because we know there were trees historically. Some areas are not suitable for planting trees anymore because the peat depth is too deep, so we leave that for peatland restoration.'

I was reminded of Cathy's work.

Innes continued, 'Maybe because of the altitude, this is a more challenging environment . . .'

He glanced over at me. My face was expressionless. He let out a big sigh. 'I see it every day. This is your first time visiting the place, and hopefully you're a bit excited by what you're seeing and what the future holds, but it's going to take 100 to 200 years.'

I wasn't feeling excited; I was despondent.

Innes continued. 'I'm trying to have a positive outlook: we'll plant more trees. I'm just trying to create a seed source. We've got nothing. In 50 years' time, someone will come in here and chop some of these trees down, thin it, leave them to rot and create a habitat. Deer will be back, cattle will be in it. This is just a stepping-stone, we're just a moment in time here.'

I could tell that what he was saying had been shaped by years of interactions with ecologists, conservationists, journalists and, of course, day guests like myself. I had the sense that Innes was trying to work out which of those perspectives I was more interested in.

I knew his background was in stalking. 'Look, rewilding is great,' I said, 'I get it, but I think we put too much of the blame on deer.'

He inhaled deeply. 'I'm not damning the deer. Our ancestors helped make it look like this.' He gestured out towards the glen. 'Of course the deer have nipped the saplings, but they've adapted to live on open range here, and we should show deer more respect, you know.'

I nodded in agreement.

'I want the deer and the trees to work together, and ultimately, all this tree planting is going to help put deer back where they belong. Deer are a forest animal: we just bred the forest out of them.'

Those were the words of a deerstalker. Tree planting wasn't a goal in itself. For Innes, it was about returning what we took from the deer: their forests.

Since restoration became the agenda at Alladale, Innes and his team have reduced the deer population from over 26 per square kilometre down to five. There were between 2,500 to 3,000 deer in the early nineties, and as a result they experienced high levels of mortality during tough winters, with deaths from starvation. Despite the lower deer density now, though, Innes can distinguish areas within Alladale where more flexibility is needed – areas that could support more deer than five per square kilometre, but also areas that need fewer.

'Am I making any sense? Am I just talking shite?' Innes asked.

He wasn't talking shite. I started to feel more at ease. Innes reminded me of some of the rural kids I had gone to school with. Maybe it was the familiar accent. Unlike some other stalkers and keepers, he was more than capable of speaking up for himself and his colleagues. Innes told me that he had sat through entire NatureScot meetings where his counterparts from other estates didn't say a word. After the meetings concluded, however, they'd gravitate towards him and voice their concerns.

Ultimately Innes wanted to see more wildlife at Alladale; he wanted to improve the land and not leave it as he found it 30-odd years ago when he first arrived on the estate. Innes stressed again that our ancestors helped sanitise the landscape that surrounded us, that they took and took from the land. He seemed to be referring to shared ancestors. Whilst Peter, Cathy and even Jeremy had acknowledged the same thing, it felt like Innes took a different kind of ownership over that legacy. Perhaps this was because he might also have come from a line of gamekeepers, crofters or cotters, but I wondered if he might also be referring to more ominous predecessors. We were in Sutherland, after all, and Alladale itself still held the weight of the Clearances. Not far from the estate was Croick church, where, etched into the glass windows, were messages supposedly written by those seeking refuge in the churchyard after being cleared from a nearby glen.

As if on cue, we passed the stone footprint of what was once a building. 'It's an old dwelling from the Clearances, possibly 1850s,' Innes explained. 'We cleared all the people to make way for thousands of sheep, and we would have just set fire to everything continually to get all the nice young vegetation all the time. Again, people are too quick to blame the deer.'

I began to understand more fully how ecologically devastating the Clearances had been, in addition to the social consequences. But I noticed my resistance to that collective 'we' that Innes used.

Innes then moved onto the scale of the climate emergency. The dominant issue for him was human population. He gave me some statistics about global population growth over the last 100 years and discussed how we needed to behave differently in order to look after land. In a nutshell, if we looked after the land – planted trees, rewetted peat, stored carbon – the land would look after us.

We'd been parked up overlooking the guest accommodation for 30 minutes, and I was desperate to see the rest of Alladale. Innes started up the engine, and we slowly crept along the track. He slipped again into tour-guide mode and told me about the old lodge in the glen that burnt down in 1875. We followed the River Alladale, and he pointed out the small pockets of natural regeneration. 'Though it's actually unnatural regen, because we've removed the deer, so there's zero browsing.'

I appreciated his differentiation between natural and unnatural 'natural' regeneration. The reduced level of browsing had raised Innes's concerns around wildfires and accidental fires, especially with the particularly dry summer.

'People are anti-burning, but a fire's a natural thing. We should use fire as a tool in our toolbox, create firebreaks, create mosaics of habitat.' Burning old heather could make way for more blaeberries in the right places. Indeed, some of Innes's neighbours made use of burning, and he could see that they hadn't caused extreme damage. It could even lead to more areas suitable for tree regeneration.

I told him that I'd only recently heard this alternative view of muirburn or cold burn.

'Everyone just looks at the negative. I hold my hands up. There are areas where we've done too much burning historically.' He held up his hands and brought the Land Rover to a stop as if to punctuate the point. 'Maybe there don't need to be quite so many grouse moors: that we can probably all agree on, but look at the habitats, look at the grouse, look at the wading birds. What's so bad about that? That's a special habitat in itself.'

He went on. 'I hate that you're recording this, but I'll say it anyway. Historically, the way this land was valued was in what it could produce: stalked stag numbers, fish caught, braces of grouse. It was how much we could take, not how much good we were doing. Now, we're hearing about natural capital: tree cover, healthier deer, red squirrels. The way we look at landscape now is changing, and I think there might be some new landowners coming into it that want to put something back – and they can still hunt.'

I jumped in with what I realised was my first real question. 'So estates aren't valued in that way anymore?'

'They are. But natural capital is coming into play now.'

He released the handbrake, and again we crept along the track. Innes pointed out some 300-year-old trees, which were, to be honest, a modest size, mostly owing to their altitude and soil type, I guessed. He then pointed out some of the faults of a plantation they'd put in, and I assumed he'd been out with a forester recently, as he seemed to recount their conversation.

Innes could tell me the age not only of trees he was responsible for planting, but also of the unnatural and genuinely natural regeneration that was taking place in fenced-off or hard-to-reach areas. His in-depth knowledge of Alladale brought with it an uncomfortable truth: rewilding takes a long time. There's a saying that the best time to plant a tree was 30 years ago, but that was exactly what Innes had done. 'Some people say there's no such thing as a tree line,' he said. 'But I'm finding there is at the moment. At Alladale, it's 400 to 450 metres. It's a challenge to grow anything above that here, so don't compare us to the Cairngorms.'

I thought of Jeremy and how enthused he was about the upward march of the Cairngorms' tree line, the altitudinal limit that a tree can survive and regenerate at. Alladale's much lower tree line made for a tantalising ecological mystery.

As we moved deeper into the glen, I noticed a line of fencing that scaled the face of a hill before cutting horizontally across

Alladale's altitudinal tree line. I asked Innes why fences were so controversial in land management. Innes took another big breath and was about to answer when we came across some other guests that had been taken on a tour by one of Innes's colleagues. They'd stopped on a wider part of track on Carn Alladale, where Innes usually likes to stop. I can see why. From there you looked right down Glen Alladale between the hills Sròn Gun Aran and Meall nam Fuaran which, further down the glen, meet the cliffs of Leacann Ghorm. Leacann Ghorm, Innes told me, is the very centre of Alladale, and from its peak you could see both the east and west coasts of Scotland, from the North Sea to the Minch. We drove past the other guests and the viewpoint and stopped further along the track beneath Carn Alladale, about a mile before the Alladale boundary.

I tried to refine my question about the fence debate. 'Is the controversy because it's a welfare issue, or is it about creating artificial environments that exclude deer?'

'It's both, and it's aesthetic as well. When you understand the deer movements here, you realise that having to put up a fence is the cruellest thing ever. We're impacting natural move-ments. But where we are fencing, we're not creating any traps for the deer.'

I could see how the fence line I saw earlier would impact their movements. I had noticed the heather had been disturbed on the hillside where they made their way around the fencing. Innes described how they'd had situations where gates into enclosures had been left open, allowing deer in. If Innes and his team were unable to flush them out, it could result in them being culled. Innes talked about how disappointing it was to needlessly shoot them.

'It wasn't the deer's fault. They could smell there was

something better over the fence, but if you leave a gate open, that's what happens.'

Despite the unfortunate trade-offs, for Innes, fences were necessary to speed up ecological recovery and get deer back into the forest sooner. The neighbouring estates had previously expressed concern around Alladale's high cull numbers and how it would impact their deer numbers – and ultimately the value of their estates. Innes acknowledged that of course there was an impact, but those neighbouring estates had maintained the deer capacity for stalking. Yet he was also aware that in the future the surrounding estates were likely to be asked to reduce their deer numbers further. Innes could see there were still too many mouths on the ground. 'Nothing's growing.'

When Innes looked around us, he obviously saw something very different from what I saw. He could see the mistakes they'd made, the less than ideal condition of parts of the land. He seemed to have an internal critic, an inner conservationist or even academic who pointed out everything that was wrong rather than everything that was good or just fine. In his mind, he must have been constantly examining the gains and losses of every decision he and the team were likely to make. He could see the impact their choices would have on the deer and other species, as well as the other environmental factors that played a role: altitude, weather systems, peat depth, the climate crisis and community engagement, not to mention the objectives of his boss and landowner, Paul Lister.

He drew my attention to the fence line that ascended high up onto Carn Alladale and over the top. He admitted this was ambitious. 'We're wanting to see if the montane habitat changes dramatically because there are no deer up there. It's been fenced for twelve years already, and I'm not seeing a massive change. There are no dwarf willows or dwarf birches appearing up there. So you question, do we need to reduce the deer to such extreme levels? And I don't have the answers.'

I thought back to the hillside with Cathy, where we did see dwarf birch, in an area where deer numbers weren't as low as Alladale. It reinforced the importance of an established seed bank. As if reading my thoughts, Innes said, 'We do have dwarf birch here, and we are seeing them grow, but it's not exciting. That's a tree that grows a millimetre a year, so really, who's interested in that?'

I laughed out loud at Innes's wry tone, and he smiled.

'People want to see trees that grow that way.' He motioned up and down with his hand. 'But we're nowhere near the point of fixing the place. It's an ongoing management project.'

Before meeting Innes, I hadn't realised that he had preceded Paul Lister at Alladale. Lister, Innes said, saw us as primates out of control, consuming the planet. It felt like Innes's boss was speaking to me through him, and I wondered if Innes himself felt the same.

'Let's be part of the solution. Let's put something back, at scale,' he urged.

I was well aware that Paul Lister and Anders Povlsen of Glenfeshie had a friendship, and I was sure Povlsen had spent time at Alladale with Lister and Innes, but regardless I decided to confront Innes with an issue that boiled my blood.

'I totally agree with that, however . . .'

'Go on.'

'I take issue with Anders, for example . . .'

'Yup.'

'And his other businesses, and the environmental damage they're doing.'

'Oh boy! You're asking me.' He looked at the recorder in my lap. 'That would definitely have to be switched off.'

*

Some time later, we were on the move again, heading back along Glen Alladale toward the main lodge. The off-the-record conversation was understandably anodyne. Acting as a conduit between myself and super rich landowners, Innes took on board my points and offered an alternative perspective. It was similar to what Jeremy and Peter had already argued, that the intention behind the changes differentiated them from any other landowners. We talked about greenwashing, legacy and depopulation as we bumped along the rough track. I'd heard enough about landowners and their intentions, though. I wanted to speak to Innes the deerstalker again. I found the right moment to tell him that I'd been on a hind stalk. It wasn't an impressive admission to someone like Innes, but it was an invitation for him to remember back to his first stalk.

Innes took his first hind at Alladale when he was eleven or twelve, the age I was when I first tasted venison at Badaguish. He took his first stag at sixteen years old, though he'd already been out stalking with clients. He shared these memories fondly. Nowadays, he found more enjoyment taking his friends out stalking, no longer feeling the need to pull the trigger. Having stalked from such a young age with family members and eventually done it for work, stalking was a big part of Innes's identity. I thought of my own family, how it must have shaped and informed their lives. For Innes, the stalk remained a special thing. The satisfaction of stalking on the high tops. Spending the day walking kilometres. The gratification of coming across a deer that had no idea you were there. Watching everything around the deer. Waiting patiently for it to stand up. He described it as a great privilege. But most special of all was hearing the stags roar in the glens during the rut. Innes didn't want these things to be lost.

Alladale didn't offer stalking as part of its guest packages anymore. Lister stopped it because it felt contradictory to the ethos of Alladale as a wilderness reserve. Nor did it pay the bills, and, ultimately, stalking meant less to Lister culturally. Innes did take Lister out stalking in the early days, but Lister seemingly didn't have the patience for it, which I can appreciate.

'Instead, guests go hiking, do tours around the reserve, trout fishing, mountain biking or just appreciate this . . .' Innes stopped and turned off the engine. 'Peace and quiet. Seeing the stars at night. I think we've undervalued Scotland, the landscape, the experience, the clean air, but we've also undervalued the stalking side.'

Innes had stopped the Land Rover on the edge of a steep bank. I was sitting precariously at a 40-degree angle, trying not to fall into him. He turned to face me and leaned against his door, warning me that he was about to contradict himself. He believed it should cost thousands of pounds for the privilege to hunt a red stag in Scotland. But he also believed that the person in the village who couldn't afford a stalk should be able to shoot a hind with him in the winter and take it home.

I told him that this contradiction sat with me too, and that I had never had the opportunity to stalk until a couple of years ago despite being a Highlander.

'You're a Highland lassie, it's part of your cultural identity.'

Something in me shifted when Innes said this – as though I hadn't fully been acknowledging the feelings of interconnectedness I had experienced with deer up until that point.

He restarted the engine, and the guest accommodation came into view.

There were changes coming to legislation around seasonal stalking, one of them being that there would no longer be a closed season on stags. Some stalkers felt this was wrong, but as Innes saw it, there was nothing to stop those estates from stalking during only the traditional season. Same with hinds; stalkers didn't want to cull hinds out of season when they were heavily pregnant or calving. But the open season meant that authorisation would no longer be needed to cull a deer out of season should there be a welfare issue, for example.

'C'mon,' he said suddenly. 'I'll show you the wildcats.'

I gave a surprised gasp. Innes slipped easily from the Land Rover as I tried to pull myself upright and climb out of the passenger door. I marched after him down a tree-covered bank, very steep and usually muddy, by the look of it. We wound our way down, and below us I saw a series of circular enclosures, rather like mesh bell-tents or miniature circus tents, with some connected by a mesh run.

When we reached the enclosures, I carefully followed the narrow, trodden path around them. This was nothing like visiting the wildcats at the Highland Wildlife Park in Kincraig: here, it felt precious and almost clandestine. Innes carefully peered into the dense foliage of one of the enclosures. There were dark dens and raised platforms. He pointed up. From above us, a small whiskered face peered down in disdain. It was a wildcat kitten.

It was a surprise to catch a glimpse of this usually shy species, and although I felt delight at seeing the kitten, the awe was not the same as seeing an animal in the wild. As we passed other enclosures, I caught the tail end of a wildcat moving nonchalantly into denser foliage and out of sight. In the adjoining enclosure, a male wildcat stood and glared at us expectantly. I couldn't discern any particular features that made it seem more wildcat than cat.

As I'd learned at the Big Picture conference, Alladale is part of the RZSS captive breeding programme for the Scottish wildcat, which aims to strengthen the genetics of the species while in captivity and then eventually release animals into the Cairngorms. Alladale hoped to follow suit and release some wildcats in its own reserve. This was one of the stepping-stones, Innes told me, before the possible reintroduction of other species such as the lynx or even the wolf.

Innes explained that technically there is no such thing as a full Scottish wildcat anymore, owing to hybridisation with domestic cats. Alladale had a couple that were 80 per cent wildcat, which is about the best that could be bred.

I daydreamed for a moment, wondering if there might still be a full wildcat out there somewhere in the Highlands. Innes said that he hadn't seen a wildcat in this part of Scotland for at least 25 years, and he reminded me of the gamekeeper's role in their demise: their pelts were of high value, probably equivalent to a week's wage. 'They're gone,' he said. The fact he had seen them at all in the wild was remarkable to me.

After a quick look around the rest of the enclosures, we returned to the Land Rover and made our way out of Glen Alladale. We turned right to cross a small bridge over the river at a point before it joined the River Carron. Then we zigzagged up a track through woodland towards Glen Mor.

'This is an example of an old-growth forest,' Innes told me. He was back in tour-guide mode, but the monotone had gone.

'You've got your Scots pines, birches, rowans, your alders and willows. The riverbanks there have birch regen, pine regen, bit of browsing; you've blaeberry coming through the heather. This is what we're striving for.'

I could tell from his tone that the biodiversity Innes saw genuinely nourished him.

He brought us to a stop. 'This is Glen Mor, the biggest glen we've got. It looks reasonably healthy here, but the further west we go we lose the tree line completely.'

Glen Mor, to my eye, was much like Glen Alladale, except for its quantity of trees. A river, the Upper Carron, meandered through the glen. There were hills either side of us, and scree on some of the hillsides, but also more consistent tree regeneration. Again, the narrow gravel track followed the course of the river.

Innes had unconsciously slipped back into his monotone delivery, which suggested to me that he stopped here regularly with other guests and visitors. The clouds were breaking up, leaving the hills stippled with sunlight. Around us was a mix of fenced-off tree regeneration, plantations and peaty wetlands. High in the hills, areas had been sectioned off for more tree planting, and some of the corries billowed with green canopies. The mix of habitat restoration reminded Innes of a bigger point he wanted to make, and he stopped the Land Rover.

'It's not about covering the place in trees, and this is what the guys who are anti-trees and the guys who are pro-trees aren't good at. We don't seem to get the message across: we're not trying to plant the whole bloody thing, we're just trying to improve certain areas.'

Satisfied, Innes took his foot off the break, and we continued westward, deeper into the glen. We passed an area of land which Innes knew was once worked by the people who were eventually cleared. He shared anecdotes told to him by his colleagues in which day visitors held some ignorant views on the Clearances. Innes told me he couldn't tolerate that.

We passed a couple of white ponies. Similar to the Glenfeshie ponies, these two were retired from stalking. We passed over a cattle grid into another enclosure, or ex-closure, as Innes has come to term them, as if to remain mindful of the species excluded from these areas.

At this point I decided to bite the bullet, and I asked him whether he thought Alladale was ready to support wolves.

Innes let out a disappointed sigh, as though he thought I wouldn't bring it up. 'Yup. Wolves don't need trees. Lynx need trees, but wolves could be out here tomorrow. There is a deer population that would support a couple of packs of wolves.' The calm, steady monotone returned to his voice, and it seemed Lister was talking to me again through Innes. 'Did we get rid of them 400 something years ago? Yup. Did we do the right thing? Of course not: we removed a predator from the landscape. Are we ready to release wolves back into the Highlands of Scotland? The answer is no.'

It was very clear from his tone and body language that he did not want to leave room for misinterpretation.

'We propose the creation of a 50,000-acre enclosure. Twice the size of Alladale. Less than 1 per cent of the Highlands, and we use the area as an experiment. We study the impacts of the wolf on the vegetation, and on the behaviour of the deer.'

He assured me it would create more employment, with fencers, ecologists, guides, lodge staff and so on. Then he highlighted something that I believed had been totally lost in the wolf discussion. Why had wolves not arrived already? Perhaps simply because Paul Lister had yet to ask the question, to approach the government. Innes thought that day could come sooner rather than later. However, for him, wolves weren't his day-to-day priority: he had enough to be getting on with.

Even with the growing popularity of the rewilding movement, the reintroduction of apex predators provokes much debate, maybe just as much as fences do. Innes told me that there are some individuals who would rather do a slow release of wolves and avoid fences. But Alladale wanted to create a fenced reserve: if it didn't work, they would just remove the wolves, pull down the fences and go back to what they were doing before. I have to admit I found the idea of a reserve compelling. Innes told me that, in Europe, people don't have a fear of wolves coming to eat them. I'm not sure what data this statement was based on, but I realised that if wolves were released tomorrow, without confines, I *would* be scared. Though perhaps I would feel differently if I'd been raised to track and hunt.

I wondered if the concerns around wolves weren't just about the welfare of livestock but also about ourselves. An apex predator could jeopardise our ability to dominate nature so freely: it could even force us to relinquish some of the control we possessed over the natural world. But if Alladale created a fenced-in reserve, I wouldn't have to put myself within it, or in any perceived danger, if I didn't want to. Everything Innes described as Alladale's wolf vision seemed reasonable: it wasn't nearly as controversial as I'd imagined before arriving on the reserve. Innes emphasised, though, that it could only ever be an unnatural environment, a glorified zoo – because, despite the enclosure's large size, the wolves' natural range would be significantly reduced.

Innes slowed as we drove amongst Alladale's herd of Highland cattle. He pulled on the handbrake and jumped out to open a gate for us to pass through. We'd moved into deer territory. It was open, the inaccessible corries providing small havens for some adept species of tree. This was where Innes would go to hear the stags rut in autumn, their roars echoing around the closely huddled hills.

I was eager to know more about the role of gamekeepers a

century ago and their relationship with the deer forest. Innes brought us to a halt and turned to me. 'Remember, these areas are called deer forests. The forest means the same as forest anywhere, but where's the forest now? It's gone.' He leaned his forearms on the steering wheel. 'Gamekeepers 100 years ago, no disrespect, would have been glorified servants. They would have been tipping their cap and just been people of the land. They would have had a tough existence and paid a pittance for it. They wouldn't have known any different.'

It was useful to be reminded of the working dynamics my relatives would have likely experienced, though I had never confused living in the shooting lodge with Highland luxury.

'Let's not speak badly of what happened before, though.' Innes was referring to land-management practices that would be frowned upon nowadays if not already illegal. 'It was a different generation, and that's the way we did stuff. I think it would be disrespectful to turn round to a stalker who's retiring and tell him his lifetime's work has been for nothing. It was a different era. We all tipped our caps, and there's still an element of that.'

I thought back to the few interactions with my grandfather that I could remember and knew that our differing relationships to nature were painfully clear. There was a time when I watched him fill in molehills to my absolute horror – I wrongly imagined the moles suffocating underground. In hindsight, it would have been a much grimmer picture had he been trapping them.

The handbrake came off, and we continued further into Glen Mor. The ridges of the hills either side of us became gradually higher and higher. Just as Innes had said, it was very open and a total contrast to the eastern, tree-filled end of the glen. The late-summer hillsides were at their most green, though the heather looked like it was about to turn. As Innes continued to chat, I scanned the hills looking for deer, knowing their coats would be in contrast to the greener hillside scrub. After being with Cathy on the hill, I had a much better sense of what size the deer would be at this distance, and I squinted my eyes to assess any contrasting dots of colour.

I tried to impress Innes with some stalking knowledge and name-dropped a well-respected stalker who died years ago. Innes, perhaps a tiny bit impressed, went on to describe him as a classic gamekeeper and considered what he might have made of Alladale's vision.

As Innes spoke, I looked up towards a ridge above a corrie and thought I saw something. I didn't say anything, though, in case I was wrong. I squinted my eyes, and, in the heather, near the top of the ridge, I could just make out a herd of brown blobs. The right colour, the right size. Deer. Innes trailed off mid sentence, looked at me and saw how focused I was on the hill. He lifted his binoculars off the dashboard and looked toward the ridge.

'That's reassuring me,' he said as he counted about 30 stags. 'This is a rewilding property. Am I concerned by that sight? Not one bit.'

He passed me the binoculars, and I searched for the brown blobs on the ridge. I found them, a herd of stags lying in the heather looking content, their antlers sitting proud. I took some satisfaction in having identified the brown blobs for myself and from such a distance. Innes pointed out that, ten years ago, it would have been a herd of 100 stags. We agreed, though, that it was just as satisfying seeing 30.

Something about seeing the stags prompted a new thought from Innes. 'You're not going to like what I'm about to say, but I'm going to say it anyway,' he warned. 'Your great-great-grandfather had a lifestyle where he ran after your classic English gentry. I had that 30 years ago. When your great-great-grandfather retired or moved on from the estate, he didn't have a pot to piss in.' Innes said this not to upset me, but because it resonated with his own experience of once living at Alladale, before Lister.

'Everyone's thinking, you've got a house there that you live in, but I had nothing, because if that guy doesn't like me and makes me homeless, where am I going to stay? You're thinking it's great, but I had a pittance of a wage.'

Innes told me how a change of ownership could lead to estate staff such as the gamekeeper being left in a very difficult position. He described how hard it would have been to live in the shooting lodge in the winter – freezing cold, feeding the fire with peat that they'd cut and dried.

'They didn't moan: they got on with it, because they loved where they were and what they were doing. But at the end of the day, they had nothing. They were working for a wealthy absentee landowner who was hopefully a great boss, but most of them were in it for themselves and their bit of sport for two months of the year.'

I absorbed everything Innes said, as difficult as it was.

He talked a little about his working relationship with Lister, which has already been well documented in television programmes and articles. Despite Lister being known as a non-traditional and even eccentric landowner with no interest in fishing or stalking, he still saw the implicit value in Innes's knowledge and expertise. As a result, Innes's role had evolved from the traditional stalker to gamekeeper to the less traditional reserve manager.

Innes talked of an alternative version of history in which, if he had been stubborn and tried to maintain the traditional ways, he and Lister might have clashed over distinctly different priorities. Innes is no stranger to criticism, often from older stalkers or other types of land managers, regarding the low deer numbers on the reserve. He might respond by pointing out that the numbers at Alladale are probably akin to what those same individuals experienced at the beginning of their careers.

The Land Rover was put into gear, and we continued along the track, leaving the stags behind.

Having read an article about the controversy around the new landowner purchasing Kinrara Estate to replant trees for carbon sequestration, I asked Innes if he knew anything about the stalkers there being laid off.

'Fuck me! I did not expect all this today,' he almost shouted.

I half apologised, quietly pleased that I'd defied his expectations.

He didn't know much about lay-offs. 'But I think the penny's dropped that, like Alladale, you can't just cover the place in trees: the trees won't grow on deep peat or along the skyline.'

The more we talked about Kinrara and the estate workers there, the more I realised how different things could have been for Innes at Alladale. The gamekeeping world was watching now with real apprehension for their livelihoods as corporate purchase of land to offset carbon increased.

At some point we crossed a small bridge over the Upper Carron, and the glen opened out dramatically in front of us. We passed Deanich Lodge, a very remote guest bunkhouse seven miles from the main lodge. Even though it was August, smoke rose steadily from one of the chimneys, and I imagined the people staying there cosied up and reading beside the log burner. This was exactly the kind of romanticisation of the Highlands that annoyed me. But it did make me suddenly realise how uncomfortable I was. We'd been in the Land Rover for nearly four hours. I was getting really hungry and I really needed to pee. Why did I keep finding myself in these situations?

We passed the lodge, and Innes pulled up off the track to let the dog out for a wander. The dog had been so quiet on the back seat, I'd completely forgotten it was there. Innes stepped out of the vehicle and leaned on the open door. I stayed put, because I could already see the midges and clegs descending. In front of us were the invisible boundaries of three neighbouring estates. The track we had been following continued south for miles and miles, crossing other estate boundaries, where it would eventually meet the road to Ullapool, near Loch Glascarnoch.

Our time together came to an end as Innes whistled for the dog, and they both jumped back in the Land Rover. He turned us round, and we headed back along the track, passing Deanich Lodge again. Innes encouraged me to chat to Lister, telling me that I would get a different perspective. Though, he warned, if I caught him on a bad day, he might say it was all over, that we'd consumed the planet. This piqued my interest: perhaps the millionaire landowner and I might possibly have something in common – our ecological grief. I turned off the recorder, and we spent another hour together, talking more about land ownership and new rural economic models as we headed back to the main lodge.

Alladale certainly recalibrated my expectations of rewilding. Maybe one day it could be a climate-crisis-mitigating biodiverse utopia, but that wouldn't be in my lifetime. And I was left with an uncomfortable feeling. Lister had been adamant about my meeting Innes. Indeed, Lister had said he would only talk to me once I'd visited Alladale for myself, and then only if Innes hadn't answered all my questions. Lister's staff were expected not only to undertake the physical labour of his vision but also the emotional, and promotional, work of explaining Alladale's ethos to people like me. At times, I'd felt as though Lister was talking to me through Innes, and I didn't like what he had to say. I couldn't help but feel that in some ways Innes and his cultural heritage were being used to legitimise or give credibility to Lister's actions within a gamekeeping Highland community. This would be in no way uncommon or unusual, but it was the explicitness of it that I found uncomfortable. I decided I had to meet Lister for myself.

Walking Drumochter Hills

My partner and I decided to stay in the Cairngorms National Park for a few days. I found somewhere that was close enough to Inverness to see family but also a short distance from the Drumochter Estate. I was excited to finally walk in Drumochter and follow the track marked on the old OS maps.

Before the walk, I had looked over the census records again, curious as to whether any further information could be gleaned about my family. I learned that my great-great-grandfather Donnie and his wife Maggie had raised at least nine children together in the Drumochter shooting lodge. I'm not sure exactly when they left Drumochter, but I know they spent at least 34 years there and eventually lived in their own home in Newtonmore. Maggie outlived her husband and reached the ripe old age of 105. Going by the old hunting adage, she must have experienced many long, drawn-out deer stalks. This was all I could learn using the available census records.

My conversations with Cathy and Innes had helped paint a picture of what it might have been like on the estate at the tail end of the Victorian era. Cathy had given me a sense of how land-management practices had impacted the ecology of the hill at the time, and Innes gave me more insight into what their working lives may have been like as estate workers. I wondered if the hills themselves would tell me anything.

It was expected to be a very hot day, so we left early to avoid walking up to the plateau in the heat. I had double-checked the safest way to access the track from the single-carriage section of the A9, and it was easy to find space in one of the nearby laybys. I had also repeatedly checked the route on a popular hill-walking website and read other walkers' write-ups of it. Despite the track giving access to several Munros and a view of the Monadhliath Mountains, the route and plateau had been described as uninteresting, featureless and desolate. But I was undeterred: this was about more than scenic views and hill walking.

We headed to the start of the track, which also looked to provide access to the powerline. At the entrance, attached to the high deer fence, was an interpretation board. It gave some information on the species that could be found on the moor throughout the year. I read with interest the description of muirburn and the legal trapping of species such as foxes, crows and stoats. These were all practices that I knew my family must have carried out on this land in their time. There was no mention of the environmental designations, which seemed like a missed opportunity.

We made our way through the gate and onto a wide, churned-up road at the base of a mega pylon. A large flock of sheep had stopped grazing on the moor and gathered to watch us as we made our way up to the track. Siouxsie's prey drive was sparked by a curious ram, and, although she was on the lead, we moved quickly to get away from it. Siouxsie was a mixed breed, but she screamed like a Toller. A walker who had just come down off the hill looked at us disapprovingly.

For much of the way up the track, a drainage ditch lay at one side, probably to stop the track washing away in wet weather, but it also drained huge sections of peat bog. The delicate burble of run-off from the peat bog followed us up much of the hill. With such a dry summer, I couldn't help but worry about the inevitable patches of dry, eroding peat and crunchy mosses. I could already feel the heat, and the steady incline meant I had to take regular breaks. Fortunately, the sun hadn't broken through the morning cloud just yet.

The track has existed in some form since at least 1870. Older maps showed stone markers that had been placed every 200 metres or so, with several cairns along the track once at the plateau. I didn't see any of the larger stones around us, but perhaps they had been swallowed up by the peat over the last century and a half. Knowing this track existed on the estate at the same time as my family, I tried to imagine them using it.

At the time they worked on the estate, Balmorality, or the idealism of the Highlands, was rife. Drumochter is only 63 miles from Balmoral as the crow flies, so I imagined there would have been similarities in the way the land was managed. It was particularly during the Victorian era that nature came to be viewed as something other than a provider of food, shelter and livelihoods. Humans increasingly considered themselves as being outside of the ecological system and instead dominant over it. Sporting estates like Drumochter were managed for the purposes of providing the landowning elite with plenty of fish and game like salmon, deer and grouse for shooting and fishing parties during their brief visits to the Highlands.

Although Donnie and Maggie both lived on the same land,

they would have had very different experiences of it. Women like Maggie likely played second fiddle to the pursuits, achievements and needs of the men on the estate. There would have been a male denial of dependency on the invisible labour women did, and no recompense for such work. As for the land, the various habitats would have served as backdrops to the male-dominant hierarchy, with moors managed to benefit deer and grouse populations for shooting. Little seemed to have changed today.

The track was cut deep into the hillside, and, in sections, the peat rose above us on both sides. Although this created a terrible scar in the land, it fortunately meant that Siouxsie could no longer see the sheep around us. At around 650 metres, we stopped to take in our surroundings. At this height it was possible to see the very north edge of Loch Ericht. Further north, we could see the familiar shape of the hills at Crubenbeg, Glen Truim and beyond to the Monadhliath Mountains. The steady incline continued, and we met false summit after false summit. At around 700 metres I heard a bird call coming from the direction of a corrie. I wondered if it was a merlin or a dotterel, but I couldn't remember their calls well enough. After that, the heather began to recede, gradually giving way to grasses and other small alpine species. I wondered if any of them were the rare species recorded in the designation reports. It was definitely much greener than I had anticipated. We reached yet another false summit and were greeted by more sheep. Siouxsie was getting slightly less jittery around them, but we still had to distract her while we ran past. At 800 metres the track started to subtly change colour, from a grey sandy gravel to something lighter. Once we reached the plateau it was clear why. It was the site of an old quartz quarry, which probably explained why this track had been around for so long. Around us lay small chunks of quartz, with the occasional quartz boulder.

We followed the white quartz road to a fork: left for the Munro Càrn na Caim and right for A' Bhuidheanach Bheag. We headed right and stopped at a pile of rocks that looked to have been discarded from the quarry. Nearby, I noticed an old rusty iron fence post, which had long since lost its wires. I wondered if this was the boundary line between Drumochter and Atholl. Or had it once been a high-altitude deer fence, like at Alladale today? I wondered if my great-great-grandfather or his sons had maintained the fence or put the posts in place. They too would have made their way to the tops for deer stalking, and they would presumably have stalked in the snowline, like I had, crisscrossing the plateau on the lookout for a herd. Donnie must have known the topography of these hills like the back of his hand, just like the stalker Allan at Corrour had. Standing on the pile of rocks, I took it all in – the hills, my ancestors. The century between us felt like no distance at all.

The sun had burned through, and the hills were dappled with the shadows from a few remaining clouds. Miles away, the hillsides of the adjacent estates were mottled dark green with forestry plantations. I noticed how the tree line stopped at the same altitude across the hills, and realised I hadn't passed a tree since we left the roadside – not even a sapling. I looked over to the north side of the pass, where only the peaks and plateaus of other Munros were visible, with Ben Alder in the distance. Despite what the online write-ups said, it didn't look uninteresting, featureless or desolate to me. Looking further along the track I could see it was a fair distance over to the corrie associated with the *cailleach* and further still to A' Bhuidheanach Bheag. I felt satisfied, though. I didn't need to bag any Munros; I'd already found what I was looking for. We began to make our way back down.

The sun was already fierce, and there was absolutely no shade on the plateau. My walking boots were also killing me. I dreaded to think what state my heels were in, but they were at least getting some respite now that my toes were smashing into the front of my boots with every step down. The large chunky gravel rocks rolled unpredictably under our feet, and I eventually had to walk sideways. As we descended, the short tufty alpine habitat of the plateau gradually gave way again to heather. The sheep had decided it was best to avoid the dog, thankfully.

From this vantage point, I noticed a small, low, square roofless structure on the hillside. It looked overgrown, and I thought it might be the remains of a shieling. But then after 100 metres, I saw another one. I looked to the southern face of the hill, and there was a whole line of the same low structures making their way down the hill. Grouse, I thought to myself. It must be for the grouse. That bird I had heard on the way up was not the endangered merlin or dotterel but rather a grouse. I got out my OS map, and indeed, there, cutting across the contour lines, were what were labelled as 'grouse butts'. In driven grouse shooting, the guns lie in wait behind the butts as a team of beaters crosses the hill towards them, flushing out the grouse. I'd somehow forgotten this was a working estate and that we were on a grouse moor; it wasn't as easy to see the patchwork of muirburn when you were amongst it. I thought again of my family, managing the very same moor for grouse. They would have used muirburn too and trapped other species, as well as had livestock grazing the peatlands. Innes's words came back to me – *it was a different era*. Standing on the moor at that moment, though, it didn't feel that different.

The dualisms and hierarchies at play on the estate when Donnie and Maggie lived there would have meant that they could only ever assume subordinate roles within a system of oppression. This was why I was wary of the seemingly altruistic nature of rewilding landowners and 'green estates'. While these landowners sought to undo much of the ecological damage done to our landscapes over the last few centuries and were finally considering the ecological needs of the environment, deerstalkers, land managers, gamekeepers and reserve managers could still be seen as the subordinate 'other' being appropriated into the dominant culture of the landowner. This thought weighed heavily on my mind.

We neared the bottom of the track, and a very hot and tired Siouxsie headed to the burn to cool off. I couldn't help but feel that little had changed here at Drumochter or across much of Scotland. Peatland was still being drained, sheep still grazed on degraded habitats and landowners, all too often, were still absent.

Paul Lister

I had originally hoped to meet Paul Lister in person, but our plans changed, and we arranged an early-morning Zoom call. I'd been surprised at how responsive and accommodating he had been to my message asking for an interview.

Before the call, I pulled out the list of questions I'd compiled after visiting Alladale. I had only 30 minutes with him, so the more important questions were circled in case we were running out of time. I launched the call and sat awkwardly for a minute, staring at my own image fixing my hair, taking off my glasses and trying to look relaxed. Then Paul's name popped up on my screen, and I admitted him to the call. In front of me appeared an older man. He wore a green polo shirt and drank from a mug with a tartan pattern. He sat in his home in west London, in a light room, his back to a corner, the edge of a wall-mounted picture frame the only personal object visible.

As Innes had done, Paul asked me to remind him what I did and why I was talking to him. I explained as best as I could and also mentioned that I was a playwright. Tim Rice had been up to Alladale, Paul said. Did I know him? No, sadly, I replied, even though I worked in theatre, I was not personally acquainted with Sir Tim Rice. Maybe one day. Paul told me that Sir Tim Rice also owned an estate in Scotland, so they had much in common. I wasn't sure how to reply to this.

Not wanting to waste time, I scanned my list and found a question that felt the most urgent and went for it: how did ecological grief manifest for him? He was visibly surprised, and a look of uncertainty crossed his face. He thought for a moment and then told me about his first time hind stalking when he was 21. He couldn't really work out what they were doing and why they were doing it. It was of course enjoyable, being outdoors, but the gralloch was confronting, and the whole experience led him to ask questions about the breakdown of biodiversity in the UK. Innes had told me something similar, that Lister had come to the conclusion that wolves should be doing the stalking.

When Innes told me Paul wasn't into shooting, I'd assumed it was because, like me, he hadn't been exposed to it. In reality, he'd already done it and had made a clear choice about it. The image I'd created of Paul arriving at Alladale and simply disregarding its traditional practices began to shift.

Following the stalk, he had come to the realisation that the UK was one of the most nature-depleted countries in Europe, and he felt a responsibility to do something about it. On a macro level, he told me, he was very concerned about our footprint on the planet.

He paused again, and an almost melancholic expression flitted across his face. He was damning of capitalism and democracy and felt that the recent news of billionaires building rockets was evidence of how stupid people can be despite their resources. This made me think of exceptions, like Dolly Parton and her million-dollar contribution to covid-19 vaccine research. I thought about the virus ripping through the global population.

I told Paul that I was paralysed by the grief I felt; I thought this might give us a sense of commonality. He tried to offer me some hope and told me to go somewhere that gave me energy. I thought of where that place might be – the Outer Hebrides, the Inner Hebrides, the Cairngorms?

Paul suggested Patagonia, and a tiny fracture appeared in the piece of common ground that I thought we shared. He told me to remove myself from the area that makes me feel this hopelessness. For him, that meant visiting wilderness reserves across the world. I couldn't help but smile at the differing levels of privilege from which we benefit.

He told me that he spends his whole life doing things that fuel him because he's accepted Armageddon; in fact, he accepted it 20 years ago. He shifted in his seat and leaned in towards the camera on his computer. His voice changed, charged with confrontation: 'So we should be a special animal, should we? We should be one that continues on whereas others are extinct before us. What makes us special? We're in fact the least special. We're probably the least intelligent.' Once he understood that humans weren't special, he could let go of worrying about Armageddon. He sat back and rolled the sleeve of his shirt down.

I reflected on how different our experience of the end of days would likely be. Which of us would win in the war for water, for instance?

I had thought Paul might bring up the issue of population growth, and he then did so, unprompted. He boiled the issue down to its most rudimentary form: humans continue to have babies and we live longer.

He put on his spectacles, picked up a printout of an article from a broadsheet and began reading it aloud. It listed seven things you could do if you were panicking about the climate crisis. He told me he agreed with almost everything on the list with the exception of 'stop flying'.

How else, I thought, would he get to Patagonia?

'And "plant a tree". Not everyone can plant a tree,' he said. 'That's not practical.' An obvious omission, he thought, was 'stop breeding'.

I bit my tongue at this point. Many of the people I'd spoken to so far, including women, had raised the issue of overpopulation. It seemed like a convenient peg on which to hang global climate-crisis issues. Not only were women most disadvantaged by the climate crisis, but for a multitude of reasons, they were also seldom able to participate in decision-making processes associated with the crisis. To my mind, the argument for population control was dangerous. It sought to disempower women by removing our reproductive rights and taking away autonomy over our own bodies whilst also failing to challenge the real drivers of the climate crisis: corporate greed and overconsumption.

In retrospect, I wished I had challenged Paul on this. Instead, my silenced fury caused the tiny fracture of our common ground to develop into a fissure. I couldn't help but reduce the notion of population control to men telling women what to do with their bodies. I thought about the family-planning packages of sterilisation, contraception and abortion that are often forced on women in developing countries, as well as the prevalence of anti-abortion laws and movements, and half-heartedly nodded, tight-lipped. Regardless, he continued to talk about depopulation and concluded by saying that he couldn't think of anything worse than having a child.

For my own sanity, I changed the subject to Alladale and what motivated his work there. He admitted that the initial driver for him was to return wolves to Scotland, albeit in a large fenced area. Yet although this was still a goal, he was no longer obsessed with it. For him, it had gone beyond wolves. He wanted to do something that was worthwhile and different, and he was not afraid of controversy; he just wanted to do a good thing.

Paul scratched his head, and I caught a glimpse of a signet ring on his little finger.

Since he had sold MFI, he said, he had spent another 20 years in the environmental field at Alladale and hoped to continue working in that space for the next 20 years. He qualified this statement, however, by reminding me that he had numerous environmental projects to continue with across the world should he ever get bored by the pace of things in Scotland. Furthermore, he declared, if he was actually as obsessed with wolves as people thought, he would have had them at Alladale by now. He could have put them in a four-acre enclosure, but he wasn't a zookeeper, and that wasn't the vision.

I asked him what was standing in the way of his vision.

'Scale,' he replied. He needed more land. Obviously he was referring to the land around Alladale – not necessarily owning it himself, but having his neighbours share in his vision. The challenge he was facing was the traditional land-ownership model, in which a landowner has a home for their family for only six weeks a year, where they won't do anything to the land and won't contribute to the local economy. Paul believed that if you owned big property in Scotland you should put it to work. For him, that meant planting native woodland and restoring nature, but for others it was about wind farms and hydro schemes. Paul's form of eco-tourism, as he described it, is what paid the bills.

While we were on the topic of models of land ownership, I asked whether Paul had experienced accusations of neo-colonialism or had any thoughts about it himself. I was intrigued to hear his response as a person involved in environmental projects across the world, from Romania to Belize.

Paul propped up his head with the knuckles of his right hand and gently nodded.

'It's a result of capitalism,' he told me. 'Why shouldn't someone with money do something useful with it, and so what if it's in another country?'

I allowed that statement a moment to sink in.

He thought the bigger issue was private land ownership, in particular where the land is kept for private use and nothing is done with it – or worse, if habitats such as rainforests are levelled. He used examples from Belize to illustrate his point. He thought globally and acknowledged that the UK created the Commonwealth, which, he informed me, created globalisation.

I tried to wrap my head around what he was saying, and he steered the conversation back round to Alladale. He explained that the estate wasn't actually worth very much: it didn't hold high agricultural value, and it couldn't be used to expand a town. This is what made it possible to plant trees and, in turn, attract tourists. He reeled off the number of locals he employed at Alladale, but that didn't indicate the quality of life they had. I wondered about living wages, job security and workers' rights, but with five minutes left, I was determined to jump to the next circled topic on my list – the social and historical context of land. Did Lister think there was space at Alladale to acknowledge its history?

He rubbed his hand down his face and pulled his eyes wide for a moment before he rested his head on his knuckles again. 'Not really.'

With that, the fissure in our common ground became a chasm.

I tried to push him on the subject of history.

'History's been a disaster,' he replied, followed by a long silence. He didn't want to showcase history or celebrate it at Alladale; he wasn't inspired by history. Another silence. We quietly looked at each other, neither willing to fill the space between us. He eventually leaned into the camera again and told me that people didn't come to Alladale for a history lesson: they were there to be given a lesson in the future and the present, not the past. I gave him a big smile, amused by the inaccuracy of his statement: it seemed to me that the very land at Alladale was a historical record of sorts.

I tried to ask another question, but he talked over me. I must have touched a nerve, because he asked me who else I'd been speaking to – which other landowners? I felt a little chastised and tried to list them. The places and people I mentioned seemed to placate him. But his body language had changed. I could see his legs were restless; he was uncomfortable. We had three minutes left, and his eyes darted to the clock on his computer. I hoped my last question would end things on a better note. What was the urgent message he wanted people like me to take away from Alladale?

Paul considered his response. He wanted people to realise the damage they had done to our country and the work it would take to put it right. 'Understand that the landscape was not as you think it might have been. This is not Scotland 500 or 1,000 years ago, so don't be complacent and appreciate what your forefathers have done: think about what you want to do to rectify things.'

I couldn't help but smile again: that sounded an awful lot like history.

I thanked Paul for his time, and we ended the call, no longer specks on each other's horizons.

13

The Stalk, Part Four

I grip the bullet casing in my pocket as I repeat what I've just said, this time a little louder.

'I've had enough now.'

Allan stops in his tracks and looks back at me.

'Are you sure?'

'Yeah, I'm really cold.' As if I need to justify my request.

'Okay.'

With that, Allan marches off, and I follow. He takes big strides down the side of the hill, landing heavily with each step in the heather and sphagnum moss. There's no need to be quiet or stealthy now the stalk is over. My gaze is focused on my feet as I try to not lose my footing and keep up with him. I have to look up every so often to check where he is, and a few times he's veered in a different direction. I realise he's traversing various ridges and dips that aren't obvious to me. The distance between Allan and me stretches out. I assume we're heading to the hind. I stop for a moment and scan the peatland ahead. I can't see her. Any landmarks that might have been apparent from the hill above have long vanished. I start to move again, and my right leg suddenly drops. I fall forward onto the moss, hands out in front as my right leg is submerged up to my thigh in a peat bog. I let out an involuntary yell. Allan stops and comes back to check that I'm okay. The nearby Rannoch

Moor is known to have quaking bogs, which can potentially trap people, but fortunately this isn't the case here, and I just have to heave my leg out.

'Are we getting the hind?' I ask as I give my leg a jiggle to get some of the bog water off my waterproofs.

'Yes,' Allan replies.

'Do you know where she is?'

'We're almost there. Ready?' Allan starts again across the peat, but he's slowed down this time, not to allow me to keep up but because we're close to the hind. I carefully follow him, watching my footing even more closely. We reach a level area, but it's still covered in dense heathers and sphagnum moss, making it slow work to traverse.

I'm still looking at my feet when I happen upon bloody patches on the grasses. We're here. But where's the hind? Panic surges through me as I realise I must have messed up the shot. I look around to see Allan standing a few metres to the left of me. At his feet is the hind. I approach her cautiously. The light winter breeze over her fur creates the illusion of her breathing. I look to Allan for reassurance.

'She's dead,' he says as he rolls up his sleeves.

She lies in a horribly contorted position with her eyes and mouth open. She's bigger than I thought, but still young. There's no time for remorse or grief as Allan brings out his gralloching knife and pulls the quarry into position. That's what she is now, quarry, an animal hunted for food. I look on in abject horror as Allan swiftly and expertly begins the gralloch. He cuts the throat to drain its blood and cuts down its belly to remove its viscera. The steely knife shines with blood. Allan's hands disappear into the quarry and around its stomach and intestines as he heaves it all out onto the mosses. His forearms are covered in blood, the edges of his rolled-up sleeves stained.

It must still be warm, I think to myself as I stand and watch with a morbid curiosity. I don't dare ask if she was pregnant. I know she likely was. I'm not even aware if he has removed her uterus, but he must have. He pulls out the heart and holds it up for me to see.

'You got it right in the heart, would have been a quick death.'

I nod, not knowing what to say.

'The heart's completely destroyed,' he says as he examines the damage, probably checking for bullet fragments.

I look at her ruined heart. I did that, I think to myself. I took that life.

'Would you like to be blooded?' asks Allan cheerily once the gralloch is over.

'Blooded?'

'It's a tradition, after your first kill, to be blooded.'

'Okay,' I say, unaware of what this entails.

Allan puts down the knife, and I kneel down across from him with the quarry between us. He checks he has enough blood on his hands. He quickly draws a line with a bloody finger across my forehead, then down my cheeks. I am not sure whether this is to honour the kill or to celebrate a successful hunt, or if it is a rite of passage. I can feel the blood's still warm, but it quickly cools in the breeze. As Allan marks a final line on my chin, he catches my lip by accident, and I immediately taste iron in my mouth. I use the back of my hand to try to wipe the blood off my bottom lip, but I have to wet my lips to get rid of it.

With the blooding rites over, Allan takes hold of the quarry's two back legs and begins to drag it across the peatland. We eventually reach an Argo track: this must be where Ethan will meet us to pick up the quarry. I find a large rock to sit on and wait while Allan wanders over a ridge to see if he can spot another herd, or perhaps the same herd. I look across the peatlands towards the Blackwater, a sliver of silver in the distance. The sky has become a flat grey, and the frost from the morning has disappeared completely. I look back up the hill to try to see where we were, where I took the shot, but I can't read the subtle landmarks of the landscape. I look across the peatland to see where the hind fell, but again, nothing.

I hear a distant engine and look back along the Argo track towards the estate. Here comes Ethan. Allan reappears.

Tired, cold and with a wet leg, I jump in the front of the Argo as Ethan heaves the quarry into the back. I notice for the first time the little specks of dried blood flicked across the surfaces of the Argo. I can feel the hind's dried blood cracking on my skin, too. I try to rub a bit off with my fingers, and I remember how dry my lips are. I really need my lip balm, a drink and something to eat, but it's too awkward to get anything out of my bag while we're moving. I don't dare look behind me at the hind. I stare to my left towards Loch Treig or dead ahead. I don't speak.

Eventually the large white lettering of the railway sign comes into view, and I feel a sense of relief. This will soon be over. I'll soon be warm. I'll soon be able to leave.

We're back across the railway line, and Allan tells me to jump into the Land Rover. He puts the engine and the heating on for me and goes back to help Ethan load the Argo onto the trailer. I quickly flip open my bag and take a drink of water, swallow a cereal bar and put on my lip balm. I put my hands up to the warm air coming from the heater and begin to feel like myself again. Allan and Ethan join me in the Land Rover, and we make our way back along the length of Loch Ossian. As I warm up, I begin returning to myself, and I even speak.

'What kind of people normally come to hind stalk?'

'Mostly people that have done it before,' Allan says.

'Do you get the stereotypical blood-thirsty hunters that want a big trophy?'

'Sometimes for stags, but we usually have people that do it to enjoy the stalk rather than the kill itself.'

This throws me. I've never considered that people might stalk as a way to spend time on the hill. I thought that meeting the cull targets was the most important thing, that satisfaction would come from achieving those numbers, not from the act of stalking. This seems ridiculous now. I realise I've totally missed the point of the stalk.

'Do you get many women coming to do this?' I ask.

'Sometimes.'

As we bump along the road, I mention Larysa Switlyk, who made headline news hunting goats on Islay. Allan knows the incident all too well and doesn't align himself with any particular side of the argument.

'It didn't do any favours in terms of the public's perception of hunting,' he offers.

We pass through the lochside woodland, and, as if he's remembering our conversation on the way out about ecology, Allan mentions some of the species being reintroduced at Corrour, such as hedgehogs and red squirrels, particularly round Loch Ossian. I look purposefully through the windscreen at the trees as we pass, hoping to spot a glimpse of something, but of course I don't.

We arrive back at the larder, and I'm greeted again by the odour that I can't quite place. Ethan jumps out and goes about getting the hind from the Argo. I stand for a moment, not quite sure what to do. Allan invites me to follow him into the larder, a purpose-built structure with a large open doorway, a concrete floor with a drainage channel, mesh grates and a track running along the ceiling. The source of the familiar odour is suddenly apparent: skinned carcasses of deer hang on meat hooks. Allan sees that I'm startled.

'These are waiting to go to the game dealer,' he tells me.

We pass the hanging carcasses and go into a large walk-in cold storage unit at the back. The smell is even stronger, almost unbearable. Hanging on hooks are a dozen or more headless and hoofless stags and hinds still with their fur, waiting to be processed. On the wall of the freezer is a rack of antlers ranging in point count, which will be sent out or collected by their hunters when ready. We move to another cold storage room. This one contains a solitary stag head awaiting its mount. Finally, Allan shows me where they process any meat that's not going to the game dealer. The stainless steel surfaces are faultlessly clean. I spot the immaculate grinder, and it's too much for me. I'm not sure whether I should be impressed by the facilities or be asking more questions.

Allan, perhaps sensing this, asks, 'Do you like venison?'

'I do.'

'Take these away with you.' He hands me a packet of venison burgers.

I thank him, then ask if I can use the toilet. Behind the locked door, I give into the exhaustion I feel. When is this going to be over? How does a stalk usually end? Does everyone get a tour of the larder? I'm soaked to my skin, and my fingers are red raw. I remember the blooding, and I suddenly feel hugely self-conscious. Did anyone else see me like this? I look around the tiny room, but there's no mirror. I turn and bend down to the silver taps at the tiny hand basin and see a distorted bloody face reflected back at me. They've run out of soap, so all I can do is wet my hands and try to rub the blood off my face. *Out, damned spot.*

I wet some toilet roll, dragging it down my cheeks, forehead and chin. The paper starts pilling from the force of my rubbing and leaves little bits on my hands and face. I look back at my reflection in the taps. It's impossible to tell if I've got all the blood off because my face is bright red from rubbing. I eventually give up, knowing that what I've just tried to do will be obvious anyway. I decide I have to leave the estate altogether, and I think of ways to do so politely as I unlock the door.

Back in the larder, Ethan's just hung up the hind. I can't look at her. Allan's hosing down the concrete floor, pushing the blood into the drainage channel. My stomach turns when I catch Ethan out of the corner of my eye. He's removing the parts of the hind that have no value, such as the hoofs, and they sit in a small collection on the floor. This catches me off guard, and my intentions to draw this to a close as politely as possible vanish.

'I'm going to go now.'

I look straight at Allan, and he turns off the hose.

'You don't want a cup of tea?' he asks, perhaps taken aback.

'No, thanks, I'm going to get back on the road before dark.'

Is that how these things usually end? With a cup of tea?

I thank him and Ethan for the day, and Allan offers to answer any other questions I might have over email. I collect my venison burgers and quickly leave the larder, stumbling out onto the cobbled courtyard. I walk past the gamekeeper's cottage to where my car's parked.

I hold it together long enough to quickly eat some food from my packed lunch and have a sip of hot tea from my flask. I remove my boots and outer layers and get in. Then I strip off all my base layers until I'm in my underwear. I get the heaters going and grab a towel from my bag, trying to rub and dry my hands and feet to get some mobility and feeling back, enough to hold onto the steering wheel and use the pedals. My legs are wet, freezing and blotchy, so I wrap the towel around my thighs. After a few minutes, I'm tired of waiting to warm up and decide to drive away like this, my feet bare. I reverse and follow the signs back to the road. Only once the lodge is in my rear-view mirror do I let the tears come.

14

Rooting

It had been over two years since the hind stalk. I'd taken myself off to the Highlands to sit quietly in the middle of somewhere. Feelings of ecological grief had been getting the better of me again. It was winter, and I was deep in the middle of a bare broadleaf wood. Standing dormant around me were birch, rowan, alder, beech and even an old Scots pine. The understorey was light and thick with grasses and brown bracken. I could hear a burn burbling nearby and the occasional call of a buzzard. I could tell there were deer in these woods from the narrow tracks that meandered through the undergrowth and the rubs on some of the trees, though I assumed that the presence of rowan meant the deer pressure here was reasonably low. This place felt right for what I was about to do.

I was naive to think that the ecological wellbeing of land could ever be attributed to something as binary as 'good' or 'bad' estates. Or even well-managed or poorly managed ones, because even on the latter I'd witnessed rare species thriving, and well-managed estates could still experience biodiversity loss. It was naive, too, to think that planting trees was synonymous with good management and conversely muirburn with poor management. By dismissing burning outright as a land-management tool, I had failed to appreciate its potential ecological benefits, particularly in the context of the climate crisis, although the scale of grouse-moor management across Scotland still seemed extraordinarily disproportionate. The factors that contributed to my sense of whether or not an estate was well managed now included the human experience. I had come to believe that today's estates that displaced people or erased human history and culture from the land only perpetuated the neo-colonial dualisms that once hollowed out these landscapes. I couldn't help but feel that some of these places would become further entrenched as emblems of de-peopling, whether or not they were wild lands or green estates.

Drumochter Estate held no archives of the time my family lived and worked there. Although this had frustrated me, I came to realise that their lives and work were documented in the land itself. I saw them in the historical ecological damage, the burning of deep peat, the persecution of certain species, the overgrazed hills. Although this was difficult to bear, I could accept that their way of managing land was of its time, and it was necessary for their livelihoods that they met the desires of the landowner. And yet, it wasn't just of its time: ongoing biodiversity loss and degradation of land was still happening on traditionally managed sporting estates now, and land ownership was still dominated by the white male elite.

I believed that Scotland's land could benefit from the ecological intentions of organisations and estates that carry out rewilding and ecological restoration, but I feared that this would be at a cost to the people and culture of the Highlands. The dualisms and systems of oppression that existed in the male-dominated environments of land ownership and land management were still utilised and would simply evolve unless they were deconstructed.

My fears stemmed from the image I had in my head of a rewilded landscape: a place without people. Despite an awareness that our landscapes were made up of layers of human intervention and management, I still unconsciously considered humans as being outside of an ecological system. I remembered something Innes had asked me at Alladale: 'If you had Alladale, what would you do with it?'

I hadn't been able to answer him, so he had reeled off a list of things that other landowners were doing to try to eke money out of ecologically degraded or low-value agricultural estates. Then he had explained why all those things wouldn't work at Alladale.

I later realised that the question Innes had put to me placed us, as humans, outside of the ecological system of a landscape or habitat. Perhaps he should have asked what I thought the land needed, or what I thought I could give the land. Perhaps the answer would have been a seed bank like at Alladale, or a deer cull like at Glenfeshie, or the reintroduction of a keystone species like at Bamff. Or perhaps all I could offer was to move through it gently.

I still wondered why I had been drawn to hind stalking. I had believed I was doing it to understand Scotland's deer problem, to participate in an act of conservation. But once I discovered my familial connection to the practice of gamekeeping and deer stalking, I couldn't help but wonder if there was something deeper, something in my blood. The dreamer in me liked to imagine it was the *cailleach* calling me to the hill to rediscover and re-examine my relationship to deer and nature as a Highland woman. Since the stalk, I had discovered the freedom to walk the hills and tops without conquering them, the ability to be on the land and not feel like an intruder and the strength to cull and grieve deer.

Hindsight gave me the opportunity to examine the ways in which the stalk could have been different. I had been so caught up in finding a 'good' estate that I had overlooked what I really needed. I'd entered a space where I assumed I had to be active, strong and inexpressive in order to participate. I instinctively suppressed what could be regarded as 'feminine' qualities in order to negotiate the practicalities of the stalk, but there were moments during it when I needed to be expressive, weak, slow, even passive. I didn't think that I needed to stalk alongside other women to feel those things, but I needed to be a better advocate for myself and subvert my instinct to uncritically assume qualities that weren't natural to me. Perhaps an alternative approach to deer stalking exists, a space where contradictory qualities can overlap, where human identity can be conceived of without the burden of oppressive dualisms: within nature, not above it. Where the non-human isn't seen as something to be controlled.

I could no longer accept the blame placed on deer. That they bore the burden of human-engineered ecological damage was no fault of their own. We had bred them out of the woods and onto the open hill. We had created a rural economy around them and imbued them with a capital value. We had undervalued them. We had made deer our emblematic species, a Highland meme, a symbol of wilderness. We had made them into trophies that adorned the walls of lodges and luxury accommodation. We had even made them into a global export. Then we made them a pest: the enemy of rewilding projects and ecological restoration. I was fortunate to have seen the deer through the eyes of Cathy, Megan, Innes, the *cailleach* and my family. To see them as displaced woodland animals, ecologically valuable, underappreciated, self-willed and smart. This appreciation meant I could feel a tenderness towards them once again.

Back in the winter woodland, I pulled a trowel out of my

backpack. Beside me in a pot was the oak sapling that I had grown from the acorn I picked up during the conference in Stirling. I began to dig through the thick undergrowth of the forest floor, eventually reaching the soil. After the hole was dug, I took the oak, eased it out of the pot and soaked its roots in the burn, gently teasing them apart. I placed the sapling in its new home and refilled the hole, making sure it was upright. So that I could find it again, I took note of our surroundings. To the east was the Scots pine; to the west, the burn; to the north, a beech tree; and to the south, layers and layers of peat. I closed my eyes, sat quietly and put down roots. I thought about the hind, the blooding, the tops of Drumochter, the upward march of the tree line, the beech, the peat bogs, the monarch of the glen, the beavers, the *cailleach*, the warrior women, the dead. These things hadn't just changed me, they had changed my intentions. I had planted the sapling; I had chosen hope.

Acknowledgements

This book began as a few short sentences that were originally copy for a new piece of theatre I had planned to develop during 2020. Within these sentences, my editor Jamie Crawford saw something much larger. With his support and guidance, I embarked on writing my first non-fiction book; it was larger in scale and scope than anything I'd written before. Though the process was often challenging, the weekly word count saved me at a time when theatres were closed and creative projects postponed and cancelled. Thank you to Jamie and everyone at Birlinn for the opportunity and for giving me a way to navigate the pandemic.

This book would also not have been possible without the support of Nick Bone and Verity Leigh of Magnetic North Theatre. Their support, in the form of the artist attachment and Rough Mix Residency, meant I could participate in the deer cull and process the experience.

I'm hugely grateful to Allan Macleod and ghillie Ethan, for taking me out on the hills of Corrour. Allan's openness and expertise set me off on a journey to rediscover my cultural heritage, for which I'll be forever thankful. Kim Moore offered support and accompanied me to Banavie to look after Siouxsie. Thank you.

For their generosity and insights, I'd like to thank Peter

Cairns, Megan Rowland, Cathy Mayne and the women of Hind Sight, Sandra Engstrom, Jeremy Roberts, Louise Ramsay, Innes Macneill, Paul Lister, Sydney Henderson, Pip Gullett and Amelie Sumpter. Each of you patiently listened to my thoughts, worries, offered your perspectives and gave me the invaluable gift of a deepened relationship to Scotland's land, habitats and species.

Thanks to Joyce Gilbert and Ceit Langhorne, both of whom introduced me to the Cailleachan and encouraged me to go for a walk along the tops. And to Jamie Lorimer and David Overend, for facilitating the Bamff residency and allowing me to participate.

Last and most importantly of all, I'd like to thank my friends and family for their patience, guidance and encouragement: my mother and father, Barry, Stewart, Chris, Jo, Helen, Rick, Louise, John and Angus Roxburgh.